With gorgeous illustrations and stylistic  1
journey of discovery. Addressing topics (s
book offers readers a way to grapple wit 3
the creative possibilities inherent in each ,
packaged with straightforward language a. .e
the perfect starting point to embrace your inner greatness. This book is
for everyone who wants to experience more peace, joy, and Good in life.

—Rev. Dr. Judy Morley, Executive Director
Intuitively Speaking, LLC

"In *Celebrate!* Jani McCarty invites us on a journey of self-discovery,
and what an adventure this book has proven to be! As we work through
each of the lessons she presents through her seven tenets, the Ponder
This questions lend insight into our past experiences and limiting beliefs, while illuminating our own personal power that's been within us all
along. This book is a gentle reminder that each of us has the capacity to
tap into our innate gifts, thus allowing us to live out our greatest purpose
through a life of joy and fulfillment. Beautifully written and adorned
with illustrations and quotes tucked between each heartfelt message, this
interactive journey is sure to awaken and heal your inner child."

—Shanda Trofe, President at Transcendent Publishing,
Founder of Spiritual Writers Network, Author of
Write From Your Heart and *Authorpreneur*

"Whether you have just begun seeking clarity and awareness or if you've
spent years considering the lessons and gifts life provides, this book is
for you. Through Jani's engaging stories, gentle reminders, and carefully
selected quotes, you will find yourself motivated to move forward. You
will also find yourself wanting more at the end of each entry; yet it is
through Jani's powerful "ponder this" prompts that what you yearn for
is achieved. In essence, she helps us recognize that we learn and grow
when we accept Life's invitations."

—Dr. Kristie Pretti-Frontczak, Author, Researcher, and Speaker

"Jani's book is an offering to your soul that shimmers with profound insight, lessons, and messages. It's a must-read for anyone who wishes to advance their life. In the experience of reading *Celebrate!* we get to discover more of our true self thru the many life experiences of its author. Read it, learn from it and more importantly apply it... you'll be glad you did!"

—Dale Halaway, Transformational Leader,
Author of *Being Called to Change*

"Meeting and working with Jani McCarty has been one of the joys of my life. Her ability to remind each of us to celebrate life is desperately needed in our present-day world. This is certainly a book to *Celebrate!*"

—Cheri Ruskus, Author, Speaker, and Business Strategist

"With stories, quotes, and thought-provoking questions in each chapter, the reader is invited to an inner journey for their own life and how to live more fully each moment. Discover gratitude for the challenges, courage for stepping out of your comfort zone, the power of forgiveness to set you free, and much more. This is a book you can return to over and over as you open it to any page and find some gem of wisdom to inspire you."

—Patricia J. Crane, Ph.D., Speaker, Trainer, Author
of *Ordering from the Cosmic Kitchen*

Celebrate!

Celebrate!

an interactive journey
thru Life's invitations....

by Jani McCarty

Celebrate!

an interactive journey thru Life's invitations....

Copyright © 2018 by Jani McCarty

ISBN 978-1-7321719-0-9

Library of Congress Control Number: 2018906783

Illustrations by Gail Folsom Jennings

Author photo credit: Katy Moses Huggins

Published by:

Forward Movement Press
Evergreen, Colorado

Dedicated to my parents,

Les and Sue Metzger,

with gratitude for their beautiful examples

of Life well-lived

and for their generous gifts of

guidance, compassion, and love.

Like branches of a tree, we grow
in different directions
though our roots remain as one.

~ Anonymous

Contents

Preface

Most of us at one point in our lives have felt different from others. It's like we have a secret that no one else has. And although we aren't quite sure what that secret might be, we feel both awed and fearful of it at the same time.

As the middle child of three girls, I was keenly aware at an early age of feeling and being different.

Perhaps it was because I was not the eldest, the princess, nor the youngest, the baby. As the middle child, I had the freedom or the curse, of finding my own way. It was up to me to define myself and my place — not only in my family but in the world as well.

Understanding this distinction about me was the beginning of an awareness of what I call my "spirit spark!"

I somehow knew I was safe and that my Life and I belonged together. Like a water drop to the sea, I was just one twinkle in the divine light of all there is.

I had a sense of my own pulse in the rhythm of the world.

As a kid I didn't spend much time questioning thoughts like these.

I don't remember judging or being critical of my uniqueness then. I just lived in the flow of Life, observing with a sense of wonder and bounding fearlessly into the middle of it.

It made sense to me that, if this strangeness — this one-of-a-kind aspect — were true of me, then it must be true of everyone I knew.

And this truth must then extend in an unlimited way to include all living things — every human being, animal, and plant.

Each of us has some sort of circumstance we believe has directed our Life experience. It really doesn't matter what that circumstance is.

By virtue of living, we are given the opportunity to define ourselves, to make our own choices, and to take action that truly determines the direction and quality of our lives.

Each of us has a unique purpose, a sole contribution to make!

As children we just know this ....

The purpose of this book is to help us remember.

With Love & Light,

Jani McCarty

"Sometimes your only available transportation

is a leap of faith."

~ Margaret Shepard

Acknowledgments

Everyone I've known or crossed paths with deserves to be acknowledged as a contributor to this book. The extent to which each one influenced me or made an impact in my Life is unfathomable.

Gratefully I acknowledge the following for their generosity in sharing a gift of themselves in support of me and the completion of my book, *Celebrate! an interactive journey thru Life's invitations....*

HMB and Smiley, my parents ~ who, by giving me Life, unleashed the possibility of who I might become.

Cheri Ruskus ~ whose passionate marketing coaching and Victory Circles Mastermind encouraged me to write (somewhat consistently) my bi-weekly Celebrate blog. And to her son Travis, who assisted me in navigating my online presence and posted my messages to social media.

Holli Sharp ~ whose creativity, as well as technical and publishing skills delivered from her warm heart, gave birth to the initial foundation of my content and layout.

Cynthia Morris ~ whose Write On! workshops and personal coaching set a structure for me to be accountable to myself and my work, and whose encouragement and direction powered me gently forward.

Gail Folsom Jennings ~ whose intuitive spirit and immense, creative talent beautifully illustrated the essence and energy of my message.

Kristie Pretti-Frontczak ~ whose friendship and professional expertise championed me, made writing less daunting, and encouraged me to respect my work.

Family, friends, and clients ~ whose acceptance of, enthusiasm for, and interaction with my Celebrate blog, support my belief that my message is important and worth sharing.

Linda Kirkpatrick ~ whose professional editing and publishing experience made her the perfect, loving editor to enhance my manuscript. And whose friendship and objective feedback enabled my authentic voice to shine through.

Lynne Metzger and Brooke Fry, my sisters ~ who continue to honor our family, love, and the journey of Life by celebrating it with me.

Hannah and Jeremiah McCarty, my children ~ who bless me with the honor of being their mother and who continue to be my greatest teachers of love and Life.

Bryan D. McCarty ~ whose non-judgmental and loving support held steady, a solid safe place in our lives, for me to create. Thank you for continuing to be the person I choose to share my Life with ….

In addition to the wisdom and teachers featured in the book, I acknowledge the following who have made a significant contribution to my Life:

Nick Kapande, nicksprofitness.com ~ whose leadership and Peak Performance community inspired and motivated me to realign with my personal integrity and self-discipline.

Dale Halaway, dalehalaway.com ~ whose TransCovery Process® and Transformational Coaching Program empowered me with an inspirational structure for personal healing and transformational teaching.

Dr. Maria Nemeth, acecoachtraining.com ~ for her blessing of "clarity, focus, ease, and grace" and whose Forgiveness Exercise changed my Life.

Jonathan Fields, jonathanfields.com ~ whose *Good Life Project* enticed me to connect with him and Stephanie Fields at The Art of Becoming Known. Thank you for inspiring me to engage in business and Life, wholeheartedly, and for curating a tribe of amazing, awesome souls.

Leo Buscaglia, Dr. Love.

Introduction

LIFE!
Our Human Journey

An awakening ...

In the early 1980's I found Louise L. Hay's little blue book, *Heal Your Body*. I was fascinated with her idea that our thoughts and feelings could actually attract and cause *dis-ease* in our bodies. I loved that Louise offered a solution, one that she applied to "cure" her own cervical cancer.

She suggested a cure could be possible just by shifting our thoughts from focusing on our illness to consistently affirming our desired healthy state. What a simple, yet formidable, consideration!

About the same time, I learned of the Universal Law of Attraction: that the thoughts, beliefs, and vibrational energy we generate and hold within us, attract like an energetic magnet more of the same to us.

Could what I think and feel about me and everything outside of me really be responsible for creating and sustaining my experience?

In theory I was a believer. Though intrigued, I was resistant to accepting any responsibility for the "negatives" in my Life. However, the seeds were planted; and on May 19, 1988, I began to "practice these principles in all of my affairs."

Getting clean and sober proved to be one of the most monumental events of my Life! I was catapulted into an upheaval of consciousness.

This was the beginning of a major shift for me. Rather than looking outside of me for the answers, I began to listen for my own intuitive wisdom.

I could see that it wasn't the people that I blamed or the boy-friends that had abandoned me. It wasn't the judgment I felt or the opportunities that appeared to be snatched away from me. Even my perceived plethora of "the unfairness of Life" was NOT responsible for keeping me stuck and unhappy.

It was me!

It was how I showed up to participate in Life. It was my attitude and behavior in reaction to it. Most powerfully, it was my feelings and the thoughts I had about those feelings that tainted much of my experience.

As I cleared out the alcohol and drugs from my body, my sense of separation began to dissolve. In that new open and clear space, I reconnected with myself and, again, felt a part of rather than apart from.

Being responsible for my Life as it is grants me the power to change it!

I am free to make choices in how I co-create and respond to the world around me.

An acknowledgment …

I've learned we rarely make changes that heal us until the pain of enduring the present state becomes unbearable. Only then do we release our death grip on our fear and find peace in the arms of surrender.

I believe we are given teachers, mentors, and guides to support us on our path. Some are our Angels, of course; and others are those loving souls who assist us from a spiritual realm.

Perhaps most noticeable are the people who come into our physical lives to journey with us. In myriad forms of contribution they catch our attention, offer us an invitation, and help us grow.

An interaction ...

"I delight in my favorite relationship, life and me!"

~ Louise Hay

Celebrate! is an invitation to consider the clues, lessons, and gifts that Life gives to us through our everyday awareness. It requires only our agreement to be present and a willingness to receive.

This book started as a series of blog posts I made over a three-year period with the same title.

My hope in sharing this piece of me and my Life is that you will allow the quote messages, the lessons, and the insights of my experience to inspire you and motivate you to choose forward movement for yourself.

You can read this book in any order. Proceed front to back. Jump to a chapter that grabs you. Go deep into one tenet. Or skim through to find a title and quote that intrigue you.

I encourage you to give yourself permission to write your responses to the **Ponder This** questions in the book. For you to have an interactive experience, it is written in workbook form on purpose.

Consider dating each of your responses as a way to acknowledge what is true for you on a given day. Life has a miraculous tendency to evolve, and our perception and experience can't help but do the same.

Life is your declaration of the human journey.

May you travel with love and acceptance in the company of compassion, enthusiasm, and gratitude!

Jani McCarty

COURAGE

Revive your valiant warrior

"Life shrinks or expands

in proportion to one's courage."

- Anais Nin

COURAGE
Revive your valiant warrior

Courage to Change

False Sense of Security

Revive Your Valiant Warrior

Hell in the Hallway

Honor Your Freedom

Courage to Change

"God, grant me the serenity
to accept the things I cannot change,
courage to change the things I can,
and the wisdom to know the difference."

Although the actual origin of this prayer continues to be debated, many attribute it to Dr. Reinhold Niebuhr. Historical origins and versions date back to Boethius, a Roman philosopher, (480-524 AD). It was distributed during World War II to the USO; and in the early 1940s it was embraced as a recovery dogma by Alcoholics Anonymous.

This shortened version known as the Serenity Prayer is the familiar message I grew up with in our family home. My mother had a small, wooden plaque with those words, one she kept on the windowsill above our kitchen sink, and she'd recite the prayer whenever a situation called for it.

I gave my Mother a cross-stitch of the Serenity Prayer for Christmas in 1982. I remember experiencing pride and humility as she received my gift, especially as it had taken me more than eight years to finish!

Six years later, I embarked on a new personal relationship with its powerful guidance. By finding the "courage to change the things I can," I quit drinking alcohol and doing drugs on May 19th, 1988.

Each January we honor and celebrate Martin Luther King, Jr., a man who brought hope and healing to America. Of the many precious values and lessons Dr. King entrusted us with, it was his profound courage that continues to inspire me today.

It is easy to observe courage and acknowledge great bravery in the heroes and leaders of our time. Yet, what about the everyday courage that exists within each of us? How and where in your Life, do you demonstrate your courage?

Accepting what we cannot change frees us from resisting unnecessary burdens. Asking for the **courage to change** that which is within our power challenges us to take personal responsibility and action!

And it is our **inner wisdom**, when we stop long enough to listen, that clarifies for us exactly which path and what next step we are to take!

PONDER THIS

What powerful action have you taken
after finding your courage to change?

....

....

....

....

....

False Sense of Security

"It takes a lot of COURAGE to release the familiar
and seemingly secure to embrace the new, but there is
no security in what is no longer meaningful.
There is more security in the adventurous and exciting,
for in movement, there is life and in change, there is Power!"

~ Alex Cohen

Most of us can relate to something we are accustomed to that has lost its appeal or element of satisfaction. We feel indifferent about it, ignore it, or even complain about it. Yet, the thought of making a change or trying something new sends us into a mini panic or, at the very least, out of our comfort zone.

It was a fall day when I took my Jeep Overland into a local dealership for a maintenance service appointment. I always found the Overland to be spacious, powerful, and luxurious, offering a unique feature that allows the entire vehicle to lower itself down to car height for ease in getting in and out. It was a perfect vehicle for transporting my father and was convenient for loading his walker, wheelchair, or groceries. It is a solid, heavy vehicle that delivers a smooth, quiet ride. He loved it and with him, so did I.

Yet in the months prior, I'd had some different thoughts about my Jeep. While I was grateful to have it, it didn't fit in so well with trips to the barn, local jaunts, or in cramped parking lots. After celebrating my 60th birthday, I felt kind of old and matronly touring around in this big vehicle. And since my father had died, some of the very features that made this model so special to me no longer had meaning or were important.

So, while I waited at the dealership, my favorite salesperson gave me a closer look at the new models I'd noticed around town, ones with a distinct, new look — sportier and definitely cool.

He introduced me to the Jeep Trail Hawk; and as we took it for a spin, something inside of me awakened. I immediately appreciated the more rugged ride and connection to the road. This new "drive" tickled my fancy and released a dormant energy. This was FUN!

When circumstances are right for us, things progress and flow in a supportive manner. By late afternoon, feeling a bit timid yet excited, I drove home my new Trail Hawk.

I awoke the next morning feeling sick and disoriented and almost afraid to look in the garage. Sitting with my husband, Bryan, at the kitchen table, I began to list the reasons for contemplating its return. After patiently listening to me justify my feelings, he asked me one simple question. "Jani, what is the specific reason you don't like the car?"

His question helped me to zero in on my thoughts and feelings. There wasn't anything I didn't like about the Trail Hawk. I hadn't had it long enough to even know how I felt about it. It was something else. I felt vulnerable. I felt insecure. And though this new path had called to me, I felt afraid and undeserving of this new freedom. There was a tug of remorse, almost regret, at having left my Overland behind.

A bit beside myself, I decided to go to my office and let go of needing to make any decision for the moment. I allowed myself to just be with it, park it, and get focused on my first appointment. A couple of times during the day I looked out over the parking lot from the third floor just to check in on my new vehicle and to ensure it was all right. It looked good out there!

As I walked out to the Jeep at the end of the day, I noticed a new energy in my step and an eager anticipation at driving it again. Snapping my seat belt, I knew my decision was made. There would be no turning back!

Indeed, that evening I experienced new excitement and enthusiasm as I sped around Evergreen Lake in my sporty little Trail Hawk. I found myself smiling from ear to ear.

In one ultimate moment I celebrated my new sense of power when belting out at the top of my lungs, I joined Katy Perry with "you're gonna hear me ROAR ...."

PONDER THIS

How have you "ignited your joy" by stepping forward in courage?

....

....

....

....

....

Revive Your Valiant Warrior

*"Courage starts with showing up and
letting ourselves be seen."*

~ Brené Brown

Have you ever felt like staying in bed, pulling the covers over your head, and hiding from the world?

I confess this is exactly what I've done — and more than once. It was my answer to escaping what I thought was threatening me — something *out there* I just couldn't bear dealing with.

The disappointing thing is that my hiding never brought me relief at all.

It only seemed to add fuel to that part of me that was feeling vulnerable and weak.

The avoiding or hiding from things in my Life that made me feel sad or uncomfortable always led me to a place of self-loathing and disconnect.

Rather than experiencing relief, I found the energy of my feelings actually intensified in my efforts to escape.

Courage can be defined as the ability to do something that frightens us. It is the demonstration of our strength of character in the face of pain or grief.

Think back to a time where you felt really afraid yet stepped forward into the very situation that you were afraid of.

What was it that supported you to do that?

What did you tell yourself that compelled you forward?

What was the result of this brave action you took?

Susan Jeffers en-*courages* us to "Feel the fear and do it anyway."

I've learned that courage is a decision. Courage is a choice. We can always choose to show up, perhaps fearful and cowering, yet taking a stand to be seen.

There have been times while acknowledging my fear or despondent heart, I chose to move forward. And though my actions may have appeared less than graceful, I survived.

In fact, taking those shaky steps forward empowered me and filled me with self-respect.

When you find yourself getting called to the front lines of your own personal battle, you are at a turning point. You can either choose to forge forward to experience victory or hide in the trees, living in regret.

There is a Valiant Warrior in each of us.

It is our brave fighter who demonstrates our strength and determination. It is what moves forward to shield us with our true grit and unwavering personal power.

It is always our choice in every Life situation to acknowledge and celebrate the glory of our courage!

PONDER THIS

Where have you been victorious by stepping forward
rather than running away?

....

....

....

....

....

Hell in the Hallway

"When one door of happiness closes, another opens;
but often we look so long at the closed door
that we do not see the one which has been opened for us."

~ Helen Keller

I have a sign above my office door that reads: "Life begins at the end of your Comfort Zone!" Needing to be comfortable is one of the strongest driving energies that keeps us from making changes, taking risks, or experiencing and manifesting what we really want in Life.

We stay in the familiar, having the same experiences over and over again. Some of us even convince ourselves that it's not so bad — that our heath, our relationships, our daily activities, and even our contributions are good enough.

We are so accustomed to this plateau in our Life that it feels safe. Yet it can be an empty and boring existence if we hold tight to this position for years.

Denying ourselves growth and change smothers our very spirit and squeezes out the passion of our dreams.

17

Letting go of needing to be comfortable immediately frees us up for new experiences. As we lower our shield of familiar, we allow ourselves to be vulnerable and open. Liberated, we can reconnect with our courage and enthusiasm for new possibilities!

In the past, I broke out of my comfort zone by kicking and screaming. I was sure that I would drown or, at the very least, be lost. Then after treading water uncontrollably, I came up for air … and found, there, a new awareness waiting for me.

Over the years as I've learned to stop judging myself or the process, making changes has become easier, more enjoyable, and definitely more rewarding.

Still, when I am standing in the middle — that uncomfortable space between *letting go* and *embracing the new* — it can feel like oblivion, even like Hell!

No longer am I aligned with the old, and not yet am I able to recognize the new.

Spiritual teacher and author Gary Zukav offers his explanation of this experiential phenomenon of limbo:

> *"When you choose to create harmony, cooperation,*
> *sharing, and reverence for life; you activate all the parts of*
> *your personality that prevent you from creating those things*
> *so that you can recognize them and heal them, one by one,*
> *choice by choice, decision by decision, as they arise."*

When you are ready to move out from being comfortably complacent, or when you choose to let go of someone or something that no longer serves your highest good, it can be helpful to remember:

When one door closes, another door ... will open.

Yet sometimes, it's hell in the hallway!

PONDER THIS

What is one significant experience of your
hell in the hallway?

....

....

....

....

....

Honor Your Freedom

"For to be free is not merely casting off one's chains,
but to live in a way that respects and enhances
the freedom of others."

~ Nelson Mandela

In the Spring of 2017 I had the privilege of experiencing the inspiring and courageous Malala Yousafzai the young Pakistani who had been shot in the head by the Taliban just three and a half years earlier as she travelled home from school and was subsequently awarded the Nobel Peace Prize. In a packed house at Denver's Bellco Theatre, I sat mesmerized as she spoke passionately for the right of every child to go to school and for women everywhere to free their voices.

Rather than silence her, the experience fueled her unwavering dedication and brought a new world view to this oppression.

At age 10 Malala began her crusade for the rights of girls to receive an education. Her bravery, exceptional clarity, and focus to the freedom of others stirs awake something special within each of us. Her father — an unlikely advocate in their culture — championed her cause.

Every time we express our truth or take a stand for our belief, we send a ripple of freedom out into the world. When we allow ourselves to be vulnerable, to show up authentically, we claim our own freedom. With each personal, courageous, and impassioned act, we honor and acknowledge the service and sacrifice of others. We cast off self-bondage and move forward in truth and freedom.

Just as Malala, we can lead by our courageous example, elevating our own experience while enhancing the lives of others!

PONDER THIS

Where in your Life have you taken a courageous stand that has made all the difference for another?

....

....

....

....

....

FOCUS

Exercise your power to choose
Direct your attention

"The last of the Human freedoms:
to choose one's attitude in any given set of circumstances,
to choose one's own way."

~ Viktor Frankel

FOCUS

Exercise your power to choose
Direct your attention

The Power of Focus

Opportunity of Choice

Recognize the Tipping Point

Choose the Direction of Your Focus

Prioritize Self-Care

The Eagle and the Wolf

The Power of Focus

"It is the resistance to what is, that creates the suffering."

~ Buddha

For those of you who have taken a saliva test, you know what it entails. For the rest of you, I'll spare the details. It's actually a very handy test for acquiring information — and in my case, specific to my adrenal and hormonal function.

I proudly completed the test. My biggest personal challenge was the requirement I abstain from coffee, tea, and chocolate for the 24-hour period prior. Emotionally, I let go of needing my morning coffee, afternoon chocolate, and evening tea. Yet the physical reactions I experienced from their absence were surprising and unsettling. I experienced low energy in the morning and felt out of sync all day. At work, I felt fuzzy and lethargic. My day seemed difficult and confusing.

What I really wanted to do was nap or perhaps hide from the public. As I plowed on, I developed a new awareness — *I was tired.* I had been "burning the candle at both ends," as my father would say. It took the break from stimulants for me to acknowledge how much I push myself, how little rest I get, and how much energy I expel on the stress of my Life, the stress that I create!

I became aware of something else I had been doing to myself. I'd been misdirecting my focus. I'd been concentrating my time, attention, and energy on my "human-doing-ness" rather than being the human I am. For me to change, first I had to become aware and accept, rather than fight, what I discover.

There is a universal principle that states whatever we focus on expands. Slowing down allowed me to see the direction and quality of my choices.

Why is it that I require uncomfortable reminders that I am not living from my authentic place? That I am racing to compete, complete, and to be acknowledged from the outside? Why do I choose to experience dis-ease, confusion, and self-punishment when I could choose to listen within, and live out happy, joyous, and free?

I have the power to change my Life. I am the power and the one responsible for my choices. No matter at which starting block I stand, it is my choice the direction to jump, or whether to jump at all.

When a holiday season encroaches, I notice the traditional celebrations of my Life and memory being transformed. And so I have a choice. I can look longingly at the past and what was or choose to be present and embrace what is — today. Shifting my focus engages my energy and directs my power to create the experience I want.

I choose to focus on **love**.

I choose being present — I choose to acknowledge, listen, trust, and love myself. And to love my neighbor as myself. Doing unto others as I would have them do unto me!

Does that sound familiar?

And in the words of John Lennon and Paul McCartney:

Nothing you can do but you can learn how to be,
There's nothing you can know that isn't known,
Nothing you can see that isn't shown,
There's nowhere you can be that isn't where you're meant to be

It's easy.

All you need is love, love is all you need!

PONDER THIS

Where in the past month, have you misdirected your focus?

....

....

....

....

....

Where could you choose to focus now?

....

....

....

....

....

Opportunity of Choice

"Indecision is the theft of opportunity."

~ Jim Rohn

I was flipping through one of my journals not long ago and found an entry I made on March 1, 2012. During that time period I was traveling back and forth from Denver to Scottsdale quite a bit, spending time with my dad and sharing in his care with my sisters.

Each plane trip offered me a transitional bridge between what felt like "my two lives." I relished flying by myself, as it was a designated time period owned only by me. I've learned that, whenever we are in a position of being caregiver, the freedom to be alone with our thoughts or the privilege of just sitting, offering nothing, is a rare and treasured reprieve.

> Sitting on the plane, ready to take off. It has been a congested, prolonged boarding. In my quiet observation, I noticed how we all have a choice — a choice on how to respond ... react to or resist the energy of this activity.

There are those passengers who demonstrate their impatience, irritation, and judgment at the source of any delay. Some appear frustrated by conditions outside of their control. Still, others chat loud and critically of the process and of the culprits they deem responsible for the problem.

And there is the additional route taken by several passengers who freely focus on fueling their own energy to whatever the upset.

Aren't we given an "opportunity of choice" at every juncture or human interaction?"

We make choices every moment of the day regarding every aspect of our lives. Whether we are even conscious of the choices we make is a choice in itself. Life is a continuous offering of events, relationships, and situations. How we respond creates our personal Life experience. We are free to choose to take responsibility for that or not!

Underlining every moment is our choice of attitude. As human beings, we have been given free will. It is our birthright to choose what we think, believe, and how we respond to our world. We can even choose how we feel or what level of health we experience. Now that statement could activate a few of us!

Our opportunity of choice spans from deciding to become aware to choosing to remain ignorant. We can choose to be:

- kind or inconsiderate
- generous or greedy
- complimentary or critical

- engaged or unattached
- fair or unjust
- energetic or lethargic
- loving or cruel

Viewing our lives as an "opportunity of choice" can be empowering. It can also be a bit unsettling to recognize it is our every decision that paints the canvas of our lives.

In the margin of my journal entry I'd written Jim Rohn's indecision quote. Reading it again now reminded me of a little parable I'd heard years ago …. **"Not to decide, is to decide!"**

Hmm …. Sounds to me like another "opportunity of choice"!

PONDER THIS

What is one situation where you consciously chose how to respond?

....

....

....

....

....

Recognize the Tipping Point

*"Genuine happiness can only be achieved when we transform
our way of life from the unthinking pursuit of pleasure
to one committed to enriching our inner lives,
when we focus on 'being more' than simply having more."*

~ Daisaku Ikeda

Growing up in Colorado, the first of August meant we had one more month of summer vacation to enjoy. Those were the days when the school year started the day after Labor Day, and most stores, except for some gas stations, were closed on Sundays. (Yes, how could that be possible?)

These days, the beginning of August marks the tipping point — that place where summer with its relaxed schedules and attitudes dramatically shifts to a focus on fall, re-establishing routines and disciplines, and preparing for the new school year just days away.

As I reflect on the passing summer, I acknowledge the sweetness of my time spent with family and friends, riding my horse, and enjoying our puppy. Spending time communing with nature at Evergreen Lake and around this beautiful community kept my focus on the blessings of the present, my spirits lifted and my heart grateful.

One particular summer I focused on taking care of me. I paid attention to my intuition and sought new resources to support my health. I also enjoyed supporting and celebrating victories with my clients and creating a new program to implement in the fall.

What about you? Take a moment to reflect upon your summer....

PONDER THIS

What highlights will you remember from this past summer?

....

....

....

....

Did you meet any new people that were significant?

....

....

....

....

Were you successful at learning something new?

....

....

....

Where did you contribute?

....
....
....
....
....

Did you make any important decisions about your Life?

....
....
....
....
....

How did you demonstrate taking personal responsibility?

....
....
....
....
....

What desire do you want most to implement next fall?

....
....
....
....
....

Choose the Direction of Your Focus

*"When you direct your thoughts toward good,
you attract positive experiences and people into your life;
but when you focus on what isn't working,
you create even more challenging situations."*

~ Denise Linn

Life is. More is revealed. And daily we get to choose which direction to take and what attitude we contribute.

Recently I focused on refreshing and rebranding myself. As I diligently focused in this direction, people and new insights seemed to come from nowhere to present themselves to support me. I experienced renewed enthusiasm and confidence to create a new website and a different format for sharing my Celebrate blog.

We create or manifest whatever we focus on. We illicit the Law of Attraction to bring forth more like-energy to whatever it is we've placed our attention. More of the same will always come regardless of our intentions or our belief otherwise.

Our freedom lies in our power to choose.

Focus is a personal choice!

Look at the direction of your Life focus. Are you choosing to concentrate your attention, energy, and time on what you want in your Life?

Or have you been focusing on the negative? Has your attention been directed at perceiving what's wrong with a situation, a relationship, or yourself?

Take a moment to look at your Life. Choose one aspect that has been presently challenging or disappointing you. In this situation or relationship, just notice the direction of your focus.

What negative result have you continued to hold in place just by focusing on it repeatedly?

What are your thoughts and inner dialogue that continue to attract and expand your present experience?

Are you willing to make a conscious choice to shift your focus in this situation?

Could you choose to give whatever you really want permission to reveal itself?

Concentrate and pay particular attention to what that might be.

Yes, it could be this simple!

PONDER THIS

What are you ready to consciously shift your focus to?

....

....

....

....

....

Prioritize Self-Care

*"The practice of extreme self-care forces us
to make choices and decisions that honor and reflect
the true nature of our souls."*

~ Cheryl Richardson

I met Cheryl Richardson at a magical event in Tucson, AZ in February of 2013. She had partnered up with Louise Hay, both in co-authoring their book *You Can Create An Exceptional Life* and in facilitating our women's retreat sharing the same name.

The loving banter and flow between Cheryl and Louise created a supportive and fun environment. They encouraged us to examine our beliefs, behavior patterns, and attitudes in our thinking. They inspired us to entertain new and limitless possibilities for enhancing the quality of our lives.

At the time of this retreat, I was fully enmeshed in sharing with my two sisters the care of our ill and grieving father. Taking care of myself was a vague concept as I juggled living in three different places and struggled to maintain some sense of personal balance. I was still reeling from my mother's death a year and a half earlier and felt lost, alone, and empty.

So when Cheryl Richardson introduced her new book, *The Art of Extreme Self-Care, Transform Your Life One Month at a Time*, I was intrigued.

As women, we are accustomed to multitasking and demonstrating by our actions whose needs we value most. Although we might have our hair or nails done, make it to our annual doctor's appointments, or squeeze exercise into our overextended schedules, we generally have limited experience with focusing on truly caring for ourselves!

We deprive ourselves, act on "yes" when we really mean "no," care for others to the extent we neglect ourselves, hide behind obligation or fear of rejection, sometimes martyr ourselves and erode our self-esteem by tolerating others' inappropriate behavior.

Cheryl Richardson's book on extreme self-care is a Life-changing handbook that offers us 12 strategies to transform our lives one month at a time. She designed it as a practical, action-oriented program with each chapter challenging us to alter one behavior that keeps us separate from the rich, rewarding lives we are meant to live.

Although this book certainly can be read and practiced alone, I know most of us, including me, are more likely to embrace something new with the support and encouragement of others. That's why I created a workshop utilizing Cheryl's book as a foundation. I added my own insights, experiences, and exercises and included a 60-minute coaching session for personal support.

Nine brave women committed themselves to traveling with me on this 12-month extreme self-care journey. Each of us was successful in making a profound shift for ourselves by implementing one or more caring strategies.

The Art of Extreme Self-Care can inspire you to dismantle your self-sabotaging behavior. It offers a new perspective and a methodical structure of support. With daily focus, it can empower you to choose to make creative and loving changes for yourself.

PONDER THIS

Who do you know that could partner with you to practice the daily support of loving and caring for yourself?

....

....

....

....

....

The Eagle and the Wolf

"There is a great battle that rages inside me.

One side is the soaring Eagle.
Everything the eagle stands for is good and true and beautiful, and it
soars above the clouds.
Even though it dips down into the valleys,
it lays its eggs on the mountaintops.

The other side of me is the howling Wolf.
And that raging, howling wolf represents the worst that's in me.
It eats upon my downfalls and
justifies itself by its presence in the pack.

Who wins this great battle?

The one I feed…"

~ Author Unknown

THE WOLF is that part of us that lives in a constant state of trying, wanting, and needing. It operates from a feeling of fear and defensiveness.

Its primary purpose is to protect us and keep us safe when we feel threatened. And we feel threatened to some degree, every time we try something new or step into the unknown, the unfamiliar.

Our Wolf attracts negative, needy, greedy energy.

This attraction comes from its belief in lack and a need to justify itself.

Think of your Wolf as "the weeds" in the garden of your consciousness.

THE EAGLE represents the truth of who you are. It is the sum of all your parts, the One Authentic You … your highest and best self.

Your unconditioned self, the essence of your soul — ***your unique spark!***

Your Eagle is the center of your intuition, imagination, and creativity.

Your true nature is loving, allowing, and accepting.

It is the whole "you" that exists in the present.

It is the source of your passion, your humanity, and your compassion and love.

It is the conduit by which spirit manifests matter — through you.

With every Life interaction, event or situation, our free will chooses how we respond. Conscious or not, we choose our focus.

THE GOOD NEWS: Once we become aware of this, we can consciously make the higher choice.

PONDER THIS

Read aloud one question at a time. Ponder your Life
experiences as you consciously breathe...

Which memory surfaces when:

You had a need to justify your position in the pack?

....

....

....

....

....

You struggled with a situation yet held your values intact?

....

....

....

....

....

You wished you hadn't sold yourself out for
a worthless golden idol?

....

....

....

....

....

You moved forward into something new,
yet sabotaged your success with self-doubt?

....

....

....

....

....

You listened to your intuition and experienced
a great sense of satisfaction and fulfillment?

....

....

....

....

....

INTEGRITY

Emulate your stance of truth

"Deep inside our integrity sings to us
whether we are listening or not.
It is a note that only we can hear.
Eventually when life makes us ready to listen,
it will help us find our way home."

~ Rachel Naomi Remen, M.D.

51

INTEGRITY
Emulate your stance of truth

Allowing Trash To Teach

Deliberate Effort

The Integrity of Bridge Mix

Who I Am Not!

Own Your Original Medicine

Fool Me Not

Impatience Is a Clue

Don't Berate, Create!

Allowing Trash To Teach

"There is only one corner of the world you can be
certain of improving, and that's your own self."

~ Aldous Huxley

While enjoying my walk at Evergreen Lake one morning, I collected bits of trash and held them in my gloved hand until I reached the next trash receptacle. After discarding my collection, I walked freely for a time. Then, as I'd spy another cigarette butt, gum wrapper, piece of foil, or some remnant of building material, I continued with my trash detail.

As a kid, my parents taught us **"Don't be a litterbug!"** Any trash we might have or create on a picnic or while traveling in the car was to be disposed of responsibly.

Growing up in my native Colorado — the state of pristine air, water, and land — we acknowledged a sense of appreciation and pride in the beauty of our surroundings. Rarely did we see trash along the roadside or on the path at a park or campsite. Yet when we did, we knew it was our job to take care of it, which we did, without exception or comment!

I remember one of us (probably me) asking Dad why WE had to pick up somebody else's trash when it wasn't even ours in the first place. The meaning of my father's answer has stuck with me my entire Life, hence, my activity today.

"It isn't your fault when others litter. But when you find trash along your path, it then becomes your responsibility and your job to deal with it!"

As I continued along my way while making new contributions to my pile, this thought came to me: **We all participate on this path, this path we call Life. We all contribute in some way, either positively or destructively, depending on "where we are" in our own lives, and how we feel about ourselves at the moment.**

As I was pondering this thought and feeling pretty good about my contribution on that particular morning, another memory floated up. I was reminded of a different time when I was not living in alignment with my values, my truth. It was a time when I was lost, searching, and acting out destructively in the interim.

It was in the mid '80s and I was driving a "demo" while working with my father at the Chevrolet dealership. I smoked then. I adhered to the rule of No Smoking in company cars by not putting my ashes or cigarette butts in the ash tray.

Instead, I'd flick the ashes out the window and then chuck the butt out too, being sure, of course, that the area was relatively free of combustible terrain. After all, I didn't want to start a forest fire!

One such time I was driving along the road by the lake and just before turning into the business center for a hair appointment, I flipped my cigarette butt out the window.

Imagine my embarrassment when a man, clad in a cycling outfit, opened the door to the establishment, walked across the room, and in front of all the other patrons, held up my cigarette butt and exclaimed, "Excuse me, madam. I think you dropped this!"

A descriptive root word in embarrassment is also what I felt like at that moment. It contributed to my shame that day. Regardless of the other destructive behaviors I held on to for several more years, I never again threw out a cigarette butt!

Rather than pass judgment on those who originated the trash on my path this morning, I acknowledge a different focus with gratitude.

Today I live in a place of consciousness that allows me to be a positive contributor. My contribution is to take responsible action on my own path, thus, clearing the path for others to follow and enjoy.

Today, I celebrate my part!

PONDER THIS

Is there someone or some situation in your Life today
that you have been judging?
How are you contributing to the outcome?

....

....

....

....

....

Deliberate Effort

"Your relief has come in response to some deliberate effort
that you have offered.
For when you are able to consciously find relief,
then you have regained creative control
of your own experience,
and then you are on your way to wherever you wish to go."

~ Abraham-Hicks

Whether it be escape from a negative relationship, reassurance while taking a risk, or simply the alleviation of a persistent irritant, we all want to experience a sense of relief and freedom.

Yet rather than trust the clear voice of our intuition, its gift of **Good Orderly Direction**, we sometimes feign ignorance. We justify taking the easier, softer way. This particular path rarely makes us feel better or changes anything.

We lose sight of the direct correlation between our conscious participation and our ability to effect change. We fall into complacency and begin to complain that we are the victims of our situation.

The truth is we are not limited or immobilized by any circumstance. It is our state of mind and our need to judge that has us believing we are powerless.

Gandhi tells us, "Happiness is when what we think what we say and what we do are in harmony."

It is essential to actively take charge of our thoughts and the language we use with ourselves and others. It is our responsibility to be intentional in our actions, to listen for guidance of our next right step!

We need to roll up our sleeves and stay focused on what we want.

When we stay the course and are willing to do what it takes to plow forward, new possibilities and rewards abound!

And here's the really good news: When we make conscious choices and take action that honors and respects ourselves, we create and set into motion the highest and greatest good for all others, as well.

PONDER THIS

Where in your Life are you ready to consolidate your efforts
to take back your creative control?

....

....

....

....

The Integrity of Bridge Mix

"Honesty is telling other people the truth.
Integrity is telling yourself the truth."

~ Dr. Robert Holden

I must have been around eight when I tasted my first lesson of integrity. I had a sweet tooth and was known to scavenge whatever candy or sweets might be available. Rarely were we allowed candy except for on Halloween or Easter. Even then our intake was closely monitored and sanctioned.

When Mom hosted bridge was the only other time candy was in our house. It was always bridge mix and butter mints — candy for the adults.

My parents might have told this story differently, and I am sure my sisters remember it in their own way as well. Still, several days before the group was to play bridge at our house, I found the bridge mix in a brown paper bag on top of the refrigerator.

I cleverly opened the bag and took out just a couple of chocolates, thinking no one would notice. I prided myself with being clever. I made several additional visits to the bag, each time being careful to quickly pull out a few chocolates before stealthily exiting the kitchen.

So when I heard my Mother shriek, "Who ate all the Bridge Mix?" I knew it couldn't be me.

I held that "position of denial" for most of the weekend, long after the bridge game had come and gone. My parents took turns offering me opportunities to fess up, to tell the truth, to just admit that I had eaten the chocolates.

There was a small voice within me that climbed to the surface several times. It desperately wanted to be honest, to relieve the heaviness that had closed in on me and made my stomach hurt.

As I lay on my bed, curled in the fetal position from holding back the truth, I finally screamed out, "Yes it was me! I am the one who ate all the bridge mix!"

I don't know what I expected, yet my family seemed neither impressed nor interested. Only I experienced a profound shift. Only I felt this great release. I was the one who was free!

Funny thing when I look back now at that experience … I learned that telling the truth to others is really just a practice of self-preservation. When I am honest with others, I feel within me, an internal consistency. And that sense of being whole and undivided is precisely what sets me free!

PONDER THIS

What's an experience you've had
where telling the truth set you free?

....

....

....

....

....

Who I Am Not!

"Success … is knowing who you are!

~ Dr. Robert Holden

Every once in a while I need to be recharged, to be inspired anew, to reconnect with my tribe, and to step out of the rat race and into the human one.

Spending five days in San Diego with Dr. Robert Holden, taking part in his Coaching Success workshop, and being immersed in a loving conscious community successfully accomplished all of that and more.

Robert Holden was all about having "a conversation," posing challenging inquiries, and deliciously entertaining us. We welcomed new perspectives and refocused ourselves to a more engaging presence.

So much of what Robert shared was familiar to me. I recognized the truth in his instruction and his stories. I was reminded of what I know yet had forgotten. I felt encouraged to shed my coat of armor to don a cape of courage!

Knowing who we are is rediscovering our unconditioned selves. It's about reconnecting with our real selves, our original potential, our spiritual essence, that true nature that existed before we identified ourselves by outer words and the criteria of others.

We mostly live our lives as our learned selves seeing the world through the perception lens of our self-image. Our self-image is a shadow of ourselves, our ego, a conglomerate of how others have defined us, our acquired beliefs, and our own self-judgment.

I thought about …

- the ways I limit myself, the punishing language, and the messages of self-doubt that still surface
- the way I feel every time I deny my intuitive voice and make choices and decisions that don't serve me
- the times I get derailed from my goal and spiral off my path in distraction.

And then I thought about how *success feels* each time I am aligned with my true self, my unconditioned self. It is my courage, creativity, clarity, respect, motivation, enthusiasm, acknowledgment, appreciation, and love that step forward into the world … as me.

And then Robert Holden invited us to ask ourselves the question that follows.

PONDER THIS

"What is it like to be you when you're not playing a role?"

....

....

....

....

....

Own Your Original Medicine

"This is about who you are, not what you do.
Capture the essence of who you are when you show
up at your best — for whatever you do!"

~ Gail Larsen

We all have experiences in our lives that dramatically shift our path and enrich our Life as we understand it. There are those people who touch us in a way that change us forever and events that wake us up to a new connection with ourselves.

Such was my experience with Gail Larsen in May of 2016 during her four-day ***Transformational Speaking Immersion*** in Santa Fe.

http://www.realspeaking.com/training/santafelocation/

With eager and anxious anticipation, five strangers and I converged upon an enchanting pueblo. We were on a shared mission to personally realize our greatest power and to trust in the potential of our truth.

Graciously welcomed, we began our awakening. We were introduced to the concept of "original medicine," an indigenous teaching that we are born to this earth with gifts and talents that are ours and ours alone.

It's our own personal alchemy.

Gail Larsen orchestrated a brilliant structure while silently holding space for each of us to find our way. And find our way we did!

With her intuitive wisdom and gracious heart, she masterfully led the six of us back to ourselves where the stories of our lives hold our magic. This place of wholeness within our unique soul she called the Home Zone™.

From the truth and safety of our Home Zone™, we can agree to be seen for who we are, what we love, and the position we take on what really matters to us. Here is the place where we let go of our fears and our need to seek answers.

Identifying, naming, and giving voice to my "original medicine" empowered me to release my fears and fuel my passion.

I am Jani McCarty and my "original medicine" expresses as *The Heart Centered Tree Witch*. It's the name that celebrates who I am and the secret wisdom I've come to contribute!

Thank you, Gail Larsen — for touching my Life, creating our tribe, and shifting our path to higher ground!

PONDER THIS

What is one powerful personal experience you could share, where
you showed up as your best — without fear or self-judgment?

....

....

....

....

....

Fool Me Not

"Forgive, O Lord, my little jokes on Thee.
And I'll forgive Thy great big one on me."

~ Robert Frost

How did April Fool's Day get established? There are two basic explanations …. One is that April 1st was a celebration of the season's shift from winter to spring. The other was the adoption of a new calendar requested by Pope George VIII to move New Year's Day from April 1st to January 1st.

Perhaps our international collective perpetuates the celebration of this day. It supports mischief and playfulness while granting immunity from reprimand by authority.

I remember pulling pranks and tricking others as a kid — short sheeting a bed, pushing someone's nose to smell the ice cream or relaying a story that was sensationally untrue. These little antics seemed harmless enough … yet now I am not so sure.

Fool is a word that can be used as both noun and verb. There are 88 other nouns for *fool* in my Thesaurus. Nitwit, chump, numbskull are just a few. All of them are some variation of derogatory.

Using the term *fool* as a verb demonstrates actions taken to deceive, trick, mislead, or dupe. Deluding another, interfering, cheating, pretending, faking and swindling are all *fooling* activities.

There's a memory I have of one kid hurting his back when another pulled his chair away just as he sat down. Or the time when some older kids tricked another into looking foolish and how we all laughed at his misery. Even the kid that was made to look foolish laughed.

Nobody really likes to be acknowledged as a person who acts unwisely or is duped. No one truly enjoys feeling embarrassed or mocked. These days it seems that the fooling has morphed into a source of harassment and bullying.

Even the smallest sarcasm used in our everyday fooling around can be a form of ridicule or mockery.

Ultimately the joke is always on us.

What we do unto others, we do unto ourselves!

As we approach the month of April, let's make a decision to bring the fun and playfulness back into our celebration of April Fool's Day. Let's agree to be mindful of others' feelings and to be conscious of our intention.

PONDER THIS

How could you play an April Fool's joke that gives
someone a loving benefit as a result?

....

....

....

....

....

Impatience is a Clue

"When I feel impatient - it is because I have a powerful desire
— that I haven't come into alignment with yet."

~ Abraham-Hicks

Impatience. I know the feeling. In fact, impatience has become a driving force and a weighted anchor in my Life. Feeling impatient can be nerve wracking, frustrating, and annoying.

When I feel impatient, I hold my breath. Impatience is where my *mistrust of Life* lives. When I experience the feeling of impatience it is because I am unsatisfied with some aspect of my Life in the moment.

I need to get beyond what's limiting me. And the more I need to *get there*, the more impatient I feel. The more hurried I get, the more behind I become.

My feeling of impatience surfaces in a response to my ego.

I need something I don't have yet.

Whatever I want is not coming to me fast enough, in the way I want it to, or in a format I can recognize.

Louise Hay tells us *"everything happens in the perfect time/space sequence."* When I resist this idea, I project my focus into the future. I desperately want what's out there to be here now.

Maybe I'm just not ready to experience that yet ....

Pay attention the next time you notice you are feeling impatient. What are you feeling impatient about? What message could this feeling be offering you?

Could it be a clue to some unrest that lies within you at the moment?

Could you make a decision to "let go of needing" whatever that is?

Give yourself permission to be patient with yourself and the situation.

PONDER THIS

What is one situation in your Life where you felt impatient
and later recognized what that impatience was showing you?

....

....

....

....

Don't Berate, Create!

"What is Love?
Love is the absence of judgment."

~ Dalai Lama

Recently I was reminded that I own sole responsibility for my attitude and well-being. This is not a new concept. Yet with so many truths and good practices, I can still fall off the path and distort my experience by slipping into judgment.

In working with others I assist them to see where their judgment may play out in their lives and how *needing to judge* comes from a place of fear, insecurity, or wanting to be loved. It is from this awareness that a new direction and healing can come.

At times it is easier to recognize the judgment in others than boldly address my own.

As a child my parents explained why "pointing at someone" is really like shooting yourself in the foot. (I doubt that is how they put it, but that's how I remember it.) I still use the visual image of pointing to remind myself of the underlying truth in all my judgments.

When we point at someone while hissing our opinion, only our index finger actually aims this message at the recipient. Simultaneously our three other fingers direct that same energy back to us. The funny thing is it is impossible to point in any other fashion.

Learning this concept really ruined my ability to unconsciously point again. Pointing became a quick clue for me to check in with myself to assess what really might be going on.

When we criticize a person, organization, or situation, the reason for this judgment originates within us. Something they say or don't say, do or don't do, activates us. We are triggered to pull up some negative feeling or memory that we may have been harboring for years.

Often our judgment comes from something we've been unable or unwilling to accept about ourselves and our lives. This negative, emotional energy thrives under our belief that we are victims and unloved.

The greatest continuous loop of activation and negative thinking comes from the judgment we have of ourselves!

Lately we have been bombarded by extreme elements that fuel our resistance and fear. The world outside of us seems beyond our control while besieging us with challenges, oppression, and hate.

The premise of personal responsibility is not altered by the depth of our activations. For every outside trigger we have the same opportunity to choose our response. We have the ultimate circumstance to effect change.

In its simplest form, our judgment originates with an attack on our beliefs!

According to the definition given by Abraham-Hicks:

"A belief is only a thought you continue to think. A belief is a vibration that you have practiced often enough that now it is dominant and therefore comes up easily and often. A belief is a vibrational point of attraction that brings evidence of itself to you."

I believe this definition offers us clarity, hope, and direction. There is nothing from the outside being thrust upon us without our permission. When we see and can accept this, we now have a place to go with our psychological battles.

We can choose to revise our beliefs so they attract what we want and reflect the truth of who we are.

The truth is we are powerful and capable beyond measure. We can choose to take an important stand; create a viable solution; or respond with loving, positive action.

Each day our lives offer us opportunities to make real change for good. In every moment we choose whether to believe in love or fear. We have the power to let go of needing to judge anything. When we choose to let go, we open ourselves up to our creativity and boundless love.

I believe whenever we choose the path that is in the highest and greatest good for us, it is by nature in the highest and greatest good for all.

PONDER THIS

What could you let go of judging that would
empower you to respond with love?

....

....

....

....

....

COMPASSION

Cultivate kindness, acceptance, love

"The decision to be the presence of love
is the most powerful influence you can have in any situation,
in your life, and in this world."

~ Tom Carpenter

COMPASSION
Cultivate kindness, acceptance, love

My Forgiving Heart

Oh, To Belong

Take Measure of a Man

Compassion Begins at Home

Our Pathway to Love

Teach Your Children Well

Stepping into Charlie

A New World

Cultivate Personal Peace

My Forgiving Heart

"Imagine what it would be like to wake up one morning and find you have forgiven everyone, and have only feelings of appreciation and love for your life."

~ Robert Holden

Now imagine that today you make a decision to let go of whatever evidence you've been holding onto, against another.

What if you forgive others for …

- whatever you perceive they did to you?
- not knowing what you needed?
- disappointing you?
- not acknowledging you?
- showing up differently than you expected?
- not having the skills or understanding you wish they did?
- not being perfect?
- making mistakes?
- being unavailable?
- lashing out in fear and pain?
- not making you feel … loved?

Look today at your relationship with yourself, at the true nature of your heart. However you are with others directly reflects this primary relationship you have with yourself.

When you forgive yourself, you are free to forgive others. When you love and accept yourself, you easily love and accept others. Your heart is open to receive all the love that is already yours.

The way to unblock ourselves and to release self-bondage is to forgive. When we forgive, we ultimately discover the truth.

LOVE is … all there is.

PONDER THIS

What judgment have you been holding onto

that you are now willing to forgive?

....

....

....

....

....

Oh, To Belong

"Service is the final healing of isolation and loneliness.
It is the lived experience of belonging."

~ Rachel Naomi Remen, M.D.

When I first read this statement from Dr. Remen in her book *My Grandfather's Blessings, Stories of Strength, Refuge, and Belonging,* I felt a deep connection to my heart and an immense sense of relief.

To live in the experience of belonging was a notion of such promise. I remembered how being of service had carved out a place for me numerous times in my Life.

My first memory of service was that of a "helping hand." In the 1960's neighborhoods in Arvada, CO where I grew up, adopted a community service to aid children as they walked to and from school. A small poster of a white hand silhouetted on a black background was placed discreetly in front windows of the homes of families participating. The poster was a symbol, a silent code that designated support and safety if a child felt threatened or afraid.

Though I never knew of anyone who actually sought help, it was reassuring to me to see the display of "helping hands" as I road my bike through unfamiliar neighborhoods.

As a middle child, my sense of belonging came from the antics I offered.

A maverick really, I took risks, provided distraction, and entertained with my dramatic demonstrations and humorous pranks. Perhaps my biggest contribution to my sisters was the courageous or reckless habit I had of being the first to consistently dip my toe into forbidden waters.

Almost 30 years ago, I learned how the true beneficiary of my acts of service is me. In early sobriety, I was instructed by my sponsor to "be of service" at our 12-step meetings. Whether I arrived early to set up chairs, make coffee, and lay out literature or stayed after to clean up, I had to commit to consistent service each week.

Volunteering for my job of service added another level of accountability for me and gave me a sense of purpose to the group. At times when doubt or self-loathing would surface, I had my service to remind me to keep showing up.

Being of service helps us to shift our focus. It frees us from being self-absorbed and the dark spiral we can enter when feeling sorry for ourselves.

I learned the importance of giving back to the source of my support, to contribute my part, whatever that might be.

I learned the only true way to experience belonging is to include myself!

Years later, my sense of service took on a deeper meaning when the dear mother of one of my best friends died. We were all challenged in disbelief and floundering in our profound grief.

I was at a loss on how to console my friend, her father, and her family. I ended up taking charge of organizing the food, setting up, and serving the folks who came back to the house after the memorial service. I kept the plates full and the dishes cleared.

It was what I could do. It was my part to assist in loving kindness. My contribution got me through the day and I know offered support to my friend's family.

As I observe our world today there appears to be a growing sense of disconnect. Through our racing technology and orchestrated social media, many channels for human interaction appear closed to us.

Yet as in the experiences of my past, I recognize that, in every situation, each of us has something uniquely our own to contribute.

And wherever we genuinely demonstrate service, we dissolve our separateness and create bonds of relationship with others.

PONDER THIS

Where could you experience belonging by
being of service to another?

....

....

....

....

....

Take Measure of a Man

*"Only when a tree has fallen
can you take the measure of it.
It is the same with a man."*

~Anne Morrow Lindbergh

How do you take measure of a tree? Or, for that matter, of a man?

His body riddled with melanoma and given a prognosis of three to six months, my father — championed by his three daughters — made a tough decision. Hearts heavy with uncertainty, we made the decision to stop focusing on his disease; the doctors' appointments, the endless tests, the diverse opinions, and well-meaning recommendations.

No longer would we allow the cancer that was consuming his body to consume our lives as well. We shared 11 more months together — celebrating Life! When my father passed and joined our mother, we mostly rejoiced — in gratitude and peace.

I learned as a girl that you can tell the age of a tree by counting the number of rings displayed in its trunk. The tree's core is tightly wound portraying the infancy of its Life. As the tree grows, with each passing year, it expresses itself outwardly into the world,

When I think of "taking measure of a man" — my father — fragments of his rings, bond together to span a lifetime of 87 years.

Through living his Life, my father taught me about *honesty, persistence, justice, responsibility, integrity, generosity, discipline, commitment, loyalty, and love!*

Several values I learned from him float up to me now as cherished memories.

Whether it was taking out the trash, wiping down the kitchen counter, picking up litter, or raking leaves, doing a thorough and complete job was paramount.

The satisfaction of a job well done. I remember watching my dad mow the lawn in the back yard, shirtless and in his bermudas. He skillfully trimmed the grass in a systematic pattern, then moved the sprinkler every few feet, his activity synchronized to a science.

Family trips were special times where we got to have all of him! He was more tolerant of our childish energy and even enjoyed our antics. He played games with us in the pool — short man/tall man, throwing us in the air — we flew like dolphins before disappearing under the water to come back around for our next turn.

The joy of love and family. And those special dinners out with his "four girls," the adoration and devotion to my mother, his soulmate of 62 years.

Teaching me to build the perfect fire in the fireplace of our family room — beginning with bringing in the right kindling and logs from the garage, wadding single sheets of newspaper into a ball, laying the fuel out like a log cabin, and with stick matches — lighting it back to front.

And then the importance of tending the fire … oh, how I love the tending, even today — **an advantageous, lifelong skill.**

The elation of sharing a heightened perspective Allowing me to join him on the roof of our house to help adjust the weather vane — I remember feeling bigger than Life, exhilarated! Standing on top of the world, looking out over our neighborhood, I felt safe and special with my dad.

Teaching me to drive! To practice safely, he took me out on the dirt roads in the country (in those days, there were dirt roads and there was country). We were rambling along when he instructed me to turn right at the next intersection. I promptly did so, skidding on the gravel and ending up in the ditch facing the other direction.

The gift of appropriate feedback/instruction. Whether I was more afraid of what had just happened or of what my father was going to say, I don't know. Yet, in his deep, steady "learn-this-lesson" voice, he turned to me and said slowly, *"Jani, in the future; you're going to want to slow down, before you turn!"*

95

The rings of a tree tell us only the number of years the tree lived. They share nothing of its character or the story of its journey. There are no words, no manner of expression that can begin to convey the quality of a Life or the value of a man.

Certainly in my heart, my father was — and will always be — beyond measure!

Take a moment to breathe … and ask yourself:

Why do we hesitate in the present to acknowledge the greatness of our loved ones?

What is it we are waiting for before honoring and celebrating their unique contribution?

What if we made a decision today to express our love and gratitude?

PONDER THIS

With whom will you celebrate Life today?

....

....

....

....

Compassion Begins at Home

"It is easy to love the people far away.
It is not always easy to love those close to us.
It is easier to give a cup of rice to relieve hunger
than to relieve the loneliness and pain
of someone unloved in our own home.
Bring love into your home for this is where
our love for each other must start."

~ Mother Teresa

The front page of *The Denver Post* showcased both the terrible unrest in Baltimore and the philosophical debate of the horrific massacre in a Colorado theatre. As I shielded myself from reading further, my heart sank. And again I searched for some understanding in all this insanity. Then in the next moment, I experienced great sorrow for the devastation and loss in Nepal from the earthquake.

Being aware and trying to process this heavy, tragic energy made me feel overwhelmed and powerless. I've learned feeling this way creates an illusion of being separate and lost without direction. What can I do? How can I help or support those hurting?

Compassion is defined as empathy, tolerance, kindness — love.

Whenever I bring my focus back to the present, my ability to feel and express compassion and to be compassionate strengthens. The path for my contribution narrows and becomes clear.

The quote from Mother Teresa reminds me that empathizing and practicing tolerance and kindness appear easier to do with the strangers of our world.

It enables me to look past the pain and loss of my real relationships — those that I have with my family, friends, and community.

Today I can take a personal inventory of sorts.

I can choose to see *who in my family is hungry, lonely, or suffering.*

Today I can refocus my attention, time, and compassion by bringing my love home.

When I take that one small action and seize the opportunity to express kindness and empathy in the here and now, my heart breaks open and remembers its song!

PONDER THIS

What is one way you could express your loving
compassion to help heal a loved one?

....

....

....

....

....

Our Pathway to Love

"To forgive … is to set a prisoner free
and discover that the prisoner was you."

~ Lewis B. Smedes

Holidays can be challenging for many of us. For some, these special events trigger depression and resentment. These triggers are especially plentiful when we look outside of ourselves for love and acceptance.

And as long as we fuel and hold onto a resentment, we deny ourselves any real ability to receive love or be loving.

Think about someone in your Life — *it could be you*— that you have been harboring resentment toward. Focus on the first person that comes to mind.

- What specifically about them makes you feel resentful?
- How long have you felt this way?

- Did these feelings originate with this person, or have they been suppressed in you for a long time?

Your answers might surprise you!

The origin of resentment is to "re-feel." It is a continuous re-feeling over and over again of an emotionally disturbing experience or a trapped negative-thinking pattern.

Resentment toward another can be identified in negative, low vibrational emotions such as anger and spite. Resentment of self expresses itself in bitterness and remorse.

Forgiveness can free us! It frees us from our limited thinking and false beliefs. When we forgive ourselves and others, we unlock the chains that bind our hearts. Forgiveness allows us to reconnect with ourselves to the light and love of who we are.

Forgiveness is our pathway to love. Right here, right now, in the present moment … where love resides.

"Forgiveness does not erase the bitter past.
A healed memory is not a deleted memory.
Instead, forgiving what we cannot forget creates
a new way to remember.
We change the memory of our past into a hope for our future."

~ *Lewis B. Smedes*

PONDER THIS

What could change as a result of your forgiveness?

....

....

....

....

....

Teach Your Children Well

"It's not our job to toughen our children up to face a cruel and heartless world. It is our job to raise children who will make the world a little less cruel and heartless."

~ L.R. Knost

Mother had a poem from Dorothy Law Nolte hanging in our home, an excerpt of which is printed below. She referred to it often. It made a lasting impression on my heart and has directed me in raising my children.

Children Learn What They Live

If children live with criticism, they learn to condemn.
If children live with hostility, they learn to fight.
If children live with ridicule, they learn to be shy.
If children live with shame, they learn to feel guilty.
If children live with encouragement, they learn confidence.
If children live with tolerance, they learn to be patient.

Father used to tease Mother saying she wasn't very realistic and looked at the world through rose-colored glasses. I guess in a way that was true.

Mother was optimistic and always had something positive to say about everyone and every situation. She was affectionately known as *Smiley* and conveyed her love and interest in others through her generous smile and focused attention.

I remember hearing her tell our father that it was her choice to look for the good — that whatever we look for in Life, we'll find.

She probably wouldn't have related her thinking to the Law of Attraction, yet she certainly practiced positive, purposeful living.

Smiley also raised us by teaching her own rules and lessons:

It's not so much what you say, but how you say it that matters.
If you can't change the situation, change your attitude.
Everyone is entitled to his or her own opinion.
What did you learn from this?
I may not like your behavior, but I always love you.
I am sorry. I made a mistake. I didn't mean to hurt you.
Take responsibility for your actions.
Just because it's different doesn't make it wrong.

We weren't allowed to tell anyone to 'shut up,' call someone 'stupid,' or use the word 'hate.'

And rather than "I can't" … we were encouraged to say "I'll try."

If we said we were bored, we were immediately sent to the encyclopedia to look something up! Or when we asked how to spell a word, we were directed to the dictionary to find our answer.

My sisters and I often argued that this practice just didn't make sense!

One of the most important lessons our mother taught us was regarding sharing information we had heard from someone else. Before passing this information on, we must have a 'yes answer' to these three questions: *Is it true? Is it kind? Is it necessary?*

This May we celebrated another Mother's Day without Mom.

Although there continues to be a hole in my heart for her physical presence, I felt her Spirit — in the hugs and laughter that flowed freely.

And when the sadness and heaviness of grief began to creep back in, I saw Smiley's face and could hear her whisper in my ear, *"Oh honey, don't take Life so seriously."*

PONDER THIS

What is one thing you learned as a child
that still serves you today?

....

....

....

....

....

Stepping Into Charlie

There's a reason why they call it *puppy love*!

I picked up Charlie, our new puppy last Friday evening, and of course, nothing has been the same since. He is adorable and a very good pup. Still, he is a puppy and quite a double handful.

Those of you who have survived the puppy phase know the choice to move forward with a dog starts with this demanding, exhausting responsibility. Other than very little sleep and a lack of personal accomplishment, this little guy has already blessed our home and me.

Charlie will meet Bryan tonight as he gets home from his annual trip to Cancun with his father and brother. It actually has been a good opportunity for Charlie and me to bond and to begin to get into a structured schedule. HA! Charlie is doing a fine job of structuring me and my Life around his schedule.

Making the decision to expand our family has been a process. Our-beloved Ernie made his transition a year ago last December. He certainly lives among us, and we are reminded of him daily in so many ways.

Yet our home and our lives became too quiet, empty, perhaps too convenient — not unsatisfactory by any means, just not filled with that daily unconditional love and joy that only a canine partner brings.

Ernie came to us at a time when our family yearned for a balancing, loving companion and needed a source of comfort and entertainment. Along the way, he served each one of us when we needed him the most.

During our search for the next perfect dog, I saw a photo of Charlie. On paper, he met all of our criteria. Yet it was his eyes that called to me. As I studied and stared into his eyes, I saw a familiar spark, a reminiscent light of love … I sensed Ernie was reaching out from that photo of Charlie.

We made the decision … to step into Charlie. Almost immediately, the lessons and gifts began.

So, this is what I have learned:

Even Life's positive contributions can challenge and activate us. Self-doubt, insecurities, fear, and judgment run rampant in those early days of stepping into a new role, a new routine, a new way of being.

No matter how tired, confused, or frustrated we feel, it is still within us to do what is necessary. Each time I crawl out of bed, fumble to put on my boots, somehow attach his leash and successfully get him out to pee in the cold backyard, I recognize my contribution to Charlie's health and success. And it's a good thing (especially as I crawl back to bed for another 2-3 hours' surface sleep.)

Caring for another, no matter how small, is an act of kindness and compassion. The passage of time is altered and my heart is cracked open to again express itself. That part of me that is selfless, loving, and accepting shows up for Charlie. Similar to my experience when caring for my dad, our new little puppy provides new meaning and fulfillment to my Life.

Getting outside of ourselves brings us back home. The priorities of the day have definitely shifted. My focus and activity revolve around Charlie's needs and well-being. He gets me out of myself and invites me to stretch to a broader perspective while focusing on what's in front of me.

There's nothing like a puppy to give new meaning to living in the present. Charlie's energy and curiosity are exhilarating. Yet he is so fast at grabbing and chewing everything in his path, all I can do is attempt to keep up with him. There is no room for my own distractions, activities, or electronics!

Adopting Charlie into our family has been both Life challenging and enlightening. The quiet moments of connection, the sacrifice of my agenda, and the forced slower pace fuel my awareness of what truly matters and celebrate my sense of family and love.

PONDER THIS

How has your relationship with a furry friend
expanded your home and your heart?

....

....

....

....

....

A New World

"Each friend represents a world in us,
a world not born until they arrive;
and it is only by this meeting that a new world is born!"

~ Anais Nin

I believe people come into our lives on purpose. They cross our paths *with purpose*. Each brings a unique gift for us — some lesson or opportunity to crack open something new within us.

Sometimes friends' contributions can appear challenging. Their honesty and direct communication can make us feel uncomfortable, even skeptical of their intentions. They consistently — and at times irritatingly so — dare us to move out of our complacency.

These are the friends in my Life that demonstrate their love by holding me accountable to the person they know me to be. They re-mind me of who I am and encourage me to stay aligned with my path.

These are the relationships committed to the long haul. These friends act as a mirror to shatter the discrepancy between my internal truth and how I'm showing up in the world.

An unknown author described this friendship so beautifully:

"A friend is someone who knows the song in your heart,
and can sing it back to you
when you forget the words."

Short-term friends drop into our lives seemingly out of the blue.

They come to catch our attention, deliver an intangible gift, help us over a hurdle, or bless us with a new insight. For me, some of my short-term friends show up winged and bearing feathers!

Many of our friends travel Life with us through specific phases or experiences. They provide companionship and a shared "measuring stick." We take turns being leader as together we journey through whatever circumstance is presently ensconced in our lives.

With these friends, we share a connection, a partnership. We practice balancing our strengths and weaknesses, talents, and skill sets while expressing respect, love, and acceptance for the journey shared.

Often when our tandem navigation is complete, we each find a new and unique path calling to us.

We forever treasure those friends who travel with us as we expand our world and move into seeing deeper and more clearly than ever before.

The greatest world of friendship can neither be defined or contained. It is that relationship that enhances our lives by celebrating every struggle and success we experience.

Friendship in its truest form is demonstrated by one human being loving another.

"Your truest friends are the ones who will stand by you
in your darkest moments,
because they are willing to brave the shadows with you
and in your greatest moments,
because they are not afraid to let you shine."

- Nicole Yatsonsky

PONDER THIS

What new world has been awakened within you
because of your journey with a friend?

....

....

....

....

....

Cultivate Personal Peace

*"When we love ourselves, we don't hurt ourselves
and we don't hurt other people."*

~ Louise Hay

Whether these words hit home on a personal level or are far reaching in a global perspective, Louise Hay's message is clear and powerful.

The terrorist events in Paris in 2015 annihilated our sense of safety and our ability to comprehend such darkness. We look out there to our humanity in disbelief and fear while we struggle for answers. How can we end this madness? What can one person possibly do?

For some, the Thanksgiving holiday generates a similar trigger of restlessness, sadness, or anxiety. Both of these events contribute to that place where we feel disconnected and powerless.

We may find ourselves straddling between thoughts of oppressive holidays in the past and anticipating what this year's gathering might bring.

Our focus is out of whack — out of alignment.

In dealing with any disturbing or uncomfortable experience, each of us has the power to make a difference. The peace and charity we want in our lives and in our world begins with loving and accepting what is ....

When we treat ourselves with love and kindness, we can demonstrate compassion to the world.

When we let go of judging ourselves from our limiting beliefs, we can practice allowing others to be who they are.

When we let go of unrealistic expectations of ourselves and others, we find a peaceful presence to experience the gifts of the moment.

When we acknowledge our feelings as they surface, the intensity of their energy can dissipate and move out.

We can trust ourselves and our awareness.

When we let go of our resentment, we become willing to forgive.

And when we forgive ourselves and others, we celebrate the freedom that comes from love and acceptance.

PONDER THIS

What are you willing to let go of to cultivate your personal peace?

....

....

....

....

PRESENCE

Create and communicate from this now moment

*"Grace is the awareness
the Life is always lived in the present
and that getting there
really means Being here."*

-Dr Robert Holden

PRESENCE
Create and communicate from this now moment

Partnering with the Reaper

The HOW of Resolution

Release To Heal

Clear the Snow

Empowered Alignment

Partnering with the Reaper

"We don't beat 'The Reaper' by living longer.
We beat 'The Reaper' by living well and living fully."

~ Professor Randy Pausch

Years ago, I accompanied my mother to a seminar on Death & Dying at the Arvada Methodist Church. The two most remarkable breakout sessions were viewing Professor Randy Pausch's **"The Last Lecture"** and a workshop where we were introduced to **"Five Wishes."**

Many of you might remember Randy Pausch, the professor, who after being diagnosed with terminal cancer, spent the last year of his Life focusing, compiling, and sharing everything he believed about **living** — in his last lecture at Carnegie Mellon.

His lecture was entitled "Really Achieving Your Childhood Dreams." It was about the importance of overcoming obstacles, of enabling the dreams of others, and of seizing every moment … because "time is all you have … and you may find one day that you have less than you think."

I remember two questions he posed that I believe are worthwhile for each of us to consider:

> *"What wisdom would we impart to the world*
> *if we knew it was our last chance?*
> *If we had to vanish tomorrow,*
> *what would we want as our legacy?"*

The second powerful session was the introduction of **"Five Wishes."** The "Five Wishes" offer us a structured format for documenting exactly how we want to be treated if we became seriously ill. Inspired by Jim Towey who worked with Mother Teresa for 12 years, **"Five Wishes"** has been called the first "living will with heart and soul."

My mother and I spent the day learning and discussing dying and death, what was most meaningful in our lives, and what care or course of action we'd want if we became seriously ill.

Those real conversations and the sweet time we spent together live on in my heart as a cherished memory.

In keeping true to herself, my mother promptly completed her "Five Wishes" document and made sure each family member knew she stored it in the livingroom bookcase.

It was what we turned to when she died suddenly, three years later.

We were able to go right to her wishes and carry them out without argument! Her every detail, written out in her own hand, gave us some sort of comfort and direction.

And although we felt clearly robbed of more time with her, we celebrate the way she lived, reminded each day to be present with courage, curiosity, and compassion.

My intention in sharing this with you today is merely to catch your attention ... and perhaps to remind you to slow down ... to consider what is truly important and valuable in your Life.

I implore you to make conscious choices that honor who you really are and the contribution you make to others.

As Professor Pausch reminded us in his last lecture,

> **"We cannot change the cards we are dealt,
> just how we play the hand."**

It's your deal!

PONDER THIS

If your Life were to end tomorrow, what would you want to leave as your legacy?

....

....

....

....

....

Below is a link to **Five Wishes**:

agingwithdignity.org

The HOW of Resolution

*"We cannot solve our problems
with the same thinking that created them."*

~ Albert Einstein

Do you think Albert Einstein meant that our troubles are of our own making?

Could he be challenging us to look to our own thinking for the culprit?

Consider whether, in our judgment of Life's events, situations, circumstances, or relationships, we transfer our perceived limitations and fear onto that which we conceive as a problem?

Solving the problems we create in our lives needn't be so ominous.

When we understand *how* to resolve challenging issues, it can become a matter of just taking the next right step.

HOW is an acronym for honest, open, and willing.

Being *honest* means being truthful, sincere, straightforward.

Honest in our thinking clears away fabrication and embellishment to bring forth our truth as we understand it.

Being *open-minded* offers that we are unbiased, objective, and flexible. Deciding to be *open* to something new or different gives way to the next message of direction or solution just waiting for its opportunity.

Then, being *willing* to change. Willing means ready, eager, and agreeable. In our willingness, we are prepared to do something, to take action!

And because of our honesty and open-mindedness, that action generally creates our resolution.

PONDER THIS

Just for fun, look at the different aspects of your Life. Where do you perceive a problem? Choose one to focus on and hold this problem in your mind.

What solution surfaces when you allow yourself to be honest, open-minded, and willing?

Release to Heal

> "All I need to know at any given moment is revealed to me.
> My intuition is always on my side."
>
> ~ Louise Hay

In 2016 I celebrated my 28th year of Life without alcohol or drugs. Sobriety has given me a second Life chance to choose daily — to live *present, responsible, and free!*

An invitation also arrived that same week to celebrate Louise Hay's 90th birthday, October 8th, in San Diego, CA. This is one Life celebration I didn't want to miss.

In the early '80s I was introduced to Louise Hay's courage, light, and love. Louise Hay has forever changed me and my Life.

Years before I got clean and sober, she planted seeds of healing in my heart with her book ***You Can Heal Your Life.***

Her philosophy — *we each have the power to change our lives simply by changing our thoughts* — caught my attention early on.

After reading her book and hearing her speak, I developed a great trust in her. I knew there was truth in what she shared. She was the ultimate crusader for teaching us all how to love and approve of ourselves.

Rather than looking outside of ourselves for the answers to our questions and the solutions to our problems, she invited us to find that place of truth, deep inside, that is our unlimited resource.

When I stopped using alcohol and drugs to fill the emotional holes in my heart, I recognized a new freedom and a relationship with myself and a *higher power* that had always been present.

I experienced an inkling of trust in myself again. Slowly I gave that still small voice within me first some attention and then faith and acknowledgment.

I've learned that each time I take action in alignment with my inner voice, I am propelled on a path that is happy, joyous, and free.

And today, each time I hear, yet ignore, its message, I get to suffer whatever consequence is presented to help teach me a new lesson.

Several years ago on the anniversary of my sobriety, *May 19th, 1988,* I took an early morning walk down the path around Evergreen Lake. As I stood at the west end of the lake, the fog began to lift in the warmth of the sun.

I stood motionless, conscious only of my breathing and feeling humbled by the beauty that surrounded me.

My heart overflowed with gratitude for my Life and the richness of my blessings.

Slowly I raised my arms overhead and declared loudly to the world,

My inner wisdom has a voice, with Love and Light I set it free!

PONDER THIS

What great gift have you received when you listened
and trusted the voice within you?

....

....

....

....

....

Clear the Snow

"In any moment of your Life, you are choosing between love and something else."

~ Dr. Robert Holden

When we get a good snowfall, my husband and I dive right into shoveling to avoid the pain of procrastination. We've honored our unspoken agreement to immediately remove the snow off our driveway and deck for almost 32 years.

Recently the 6 inches of snow we were to receive turned out to be 14 inches instead. Although my shoveling partner was out of town, my spirits were high as I set out to do my job.

Shoveling is rather therapeutic for me. It is a way of meditation, a simple rhythmic routine. Being physically outside and breathing in the fresh, crisp air clears my head and invigorates me.

I quickly evaluated my task at hand in the early morning quiet. Today, I had the freedom to choose my own way of tackling this responsibility.

Though the sun had yet another hour before assisting me, appropriately dressed and centered in my breath, I began.

The steady, smooth swoosh of my shovel on the pavement was the only sound that echoed around me. I consciously walked each scoop over to the side of the drive and flipped it over the retaining wall onto the growing pile.

Some of my first thoughts were of my mother. I smiled and felt warm inside as I pictured her out shoveling, her green plaid scarf wrapped tightly around her head and mouth like a muzzle. She was the snow shoveler of our family.

She taught my sisters and me the fine art of clearing snow. She instilled in us an appreciation for both the beauty of snow and that great sense of accomplishment in shoveling it.

When focused on my mother and those happy memories, my shoveling was smooth, consistent, and productive. I felt a patient pleasure in the progress I was making and in the dance of my own movements.

After awhile I looked up to assess what remained to be cleared and immediately felt discouraged at the wall of snow still ahead of me.

I began to feel a bit resentful of my husband, who was enjoying himself in Mexico!

Stuck in fueling my thoughts of judgment and resentment, I started to attack the snow and fight with myself. Finally, exhausted, I stopped to catch my breath.

The sun now peeking through the trees humbled me and the fragrant scent of pine, refreshed my attitude. Reminded of the gifts that surrounded me, I felt grateful for my health and the ability to shovel in the first place.

Physically clearing the snow acts as a metaphor, a reflection of my internal journey. Three hours later I finished with my last scoop before stepping back to admire what I had accomplished.

It was a job my mom would have been proud to see!

And then I felt that *special knowing*.

She had been with me all along.

PONDER THIS

When have you stopped to take a breath and clear your snow?

....

....

....

....

....

Empowered Enlightenment

*"Once you remember who you are
and once you deliberately reach for thoughts
that hold you in vibrational alignment
with who you are,
your world will also fall into alignment
and well-being will show itself to you
in all areas of your life experience."*

~ Abraham-Hicks

To remember who you are, simply let go of focusing on who you are not.

You are not your past; your experiential memories, your conditioned self-identity, or the result of any circumstance.

You are not the depressed feeling you might experience when you replay old judgments about yourself.

Nor are you the projection of your future.

Focusing on expectations of how you and your Life might look reflects only your ego, impatiently waiting and wanting to express itself. This "future thinking" is non-serving as it fuels your perception with further distraction and discontent.

Although these aspects contribute to a physical human experience, none is our true essence. In truth, we are vibrational, spiritual energy, expressing itself through human understanding.

And we can experience no serenity when we practice projecting ourselves to a time or place other than NOW.

The great Eastern philosopher Lao Tzu, reminds us:

If we are at peace, it is because we are living in the present.

The present, this now moment, is where we reconnect and align with ourselves. It is where who we really are — and what we really are — lives.

When we experience feeling lonely, sad, or overwhelmed, we move away from the present. We are drowning in our woes of the past or frantically trying to control the future.

The most effective approach I know for coming home to the present, this place of peace, is conscious or mindful breathing.

There are many methods and breathing practices embraced by different communities and paths of study. We have our diverse Yoga breaths, the Pilates 100's breath, the 'birth-giving' pant, and the breathing rhythm best used for runners. And the breath of our Spirit — that ultimate Breath — the last to leave our bodies when we die.

I have discovered a simple, specific breathing practice that absolutely re-centers and grounds me. It is a "breezeway" of sorts between my head and heart.

Those who have worked with me know I call my specific way of mindful, deliberate breathing Exaggerated Breathing. It is perhaps my nature to embellish a good thing.

It is this same practiced breathing that gives me pause when activated and frees me up to recognize at any moment that I have the power of choice!

This way of breathing anchors me to my source, expands my experience of joy, and partners with me to celebrate Life!

EXAGGERATED BREATHING

- Step 1   Take a long, deep inhale through your nose.

- Step 2   Pause with the awareness of your breath filling and expanding your body.

- Step 3   Exhale slowly and completely through your open mouth allowing an "ahh" sound to escape as your body releases.

Once may do it. I prefer to repeat three times. Ah….

In seeking a centered self, we find alignment in our world!

PONDER THIS

What is one trigger you experience where stopping to
consciously breathe could support you to feel empowered?

....

....

....

....

....

SURRENDER

Empower your freedom by letting go

"Giving up control will be required
at one point in your journey.
Your seed must be cast into the spiraling wind,
to be picked up by the invisible lines of Higher Potential
and carried to the place
where they will become a new reality."

~ Ross Hostetter,
Keepers of the Field

SURRENDER
Empower your freedom by letting go

A Surprise Relief

Consciously Unplug

Our Fog Is Temporary

Walking the Slight Edge

Finding the Balance

Reluctant Acceptance

Letting Go Is a Process

Claim Your Freedom

A Surprise Relief

"Wholeness occurs when you can say yes to both endings and beginnings."

~ Denise Linn

My landlord called in late July to tell me my lease was up and asked what I wanted to do. Without hesitation I told him I'd renew and hung up the phone. Nothing unusual about that except almost immediately I felt unsettled and disoriented.

In the days that followed while contemplating the renewal of my lease, all sorts of conflicting messages surfaced. I vacillated between reducing the lease to one year, finding someone to rent my classroom, and deciding not to renew all together.

Where had this *uncertainty* come from? Why was I questioning my decision?

There was nothing wrong. There wasn't anything pressuring me to make a change. Yet there was *something* within me wrestling for my attention. That *something* tripped me up and left me feeling fragmented and confused.

145

I was afraid to talk about my thoughts with anyone. How could I explain? There just wasn't a clear rationale for ending something that was working, something that was good. It seemed foolish to consider making a change.

Yet over and over an undeniable voice spoke to me. It urged me to be open, to let go. It encouraged me to trust Life and embrace the ending of my "business as usual."

In the past I've resisted and ignored my intuitive voice and stubbornly pushed myself forward on an old path. Later when I found my courage, I could see the limitation and denial I had held on to.

This time I would do something different. This time, I would stay the course and go where Life led me.

Eventually my resistance and self-judgment softened. I could see that my office and classroom weren't what was real. They were extensions of me and my energy rather than the other way around. When I released the weight of my projections, the light of my heart returned. The battle was over.

I closed my Love & Light office at the end of September, 2016. When the movers loaded their truck, they took a part of my heart and the very core of the safe haven my clients and I had enjoyed for more than three years.

Still in one final gesture, I closed the door to my office and walked confidently to my car. I looked up at the sky and was filled with gratitude and a great sense of relief.

With a twinkle in my eye, I smiled and opened myself fully with enthusiastic anticipation … for what's to come!

PONDER THIS

When have you let go of something good in your Life so you could be open to something better?

....

....

....

....

....

Consciously Unplug

"Surrendering to what is ... frees the answer to what's next."

~ Sambo Reigns

Recently I found myself feeling assaulted and then defensive. It's my response to the disrespectful and negative energies being perpetuated onto our humanity and to our precious Mother Earth.

Lives slaughtered, anger, resentment, and fear viciously demonstrated, is both senseless and incomprehensible. With each new account I felt more powerless and depleted. It was difficult to breathe.

In my everyday activities I found an endless stream of fresh trash and garbage everywhere I went. Whether at the Rec Center, the bike park, the grocery store parking lot, or Evergreen Lake, there was a total disregard for personal responsibility and preservation.

I found myself disheartened by the dog poop and cigarette butts bordering all my favorite and familiar trails. The excess of it all snatched my attention and forced me to disregard the beauty that was still there, peeking through.

I continued to pick up trash while making condescending re-marks about the dog owners and the health of the nicotine addicts. At one point I found myself laughing at how awful it all was and then really "needing to do something" about it!

Finally I recognized what was happening. I saw that my focus on all this dark energy had distracted and derailed me. I saw that I was now resisting doing my own part and had joined the ranks of "feeling resentful and angry."

Awareness is such a powerful ally! In this instance it stopped me in my tracks and demanded to be acknowledged. I took a long, deep breath, regrouped, and listened. Like a bolt of lightening, I saw the next right steps before me. They immediately helped me realign with my serenity, gratitude, and acceptance.

Try these 3 Life-saving steps for yourself:

1. **Unplug from the hype**. Whether it is the news, facebook, email, criticism, or someone else's drama — if it is unsettling, move away. Let go of being a captive audience. Unplug your-self from the connection! A client shared with me recently about her experience with listening to National Public Radio. She said she had always enjoyed listening in until now. She found every time she tuned in these days, she felt anxious and frustrated. Rather than accompanying her while she worked, she found it to be distracting and uncomfortable. She made a decision to just unplug for a few days. Good idea.

2. **Give yourself a time out.** Give yourself permission to sit this one out for a bit. What if you gave yourself an extra five minutes in the shower to luxuriate in the soothing water and your gratitude? What if you just didn't go to that event or party? How would it feel to stay home in your loungewear? You could read, watch a movie, or even have a meaningful conversation with a loved one.

   What if you gave yourself permission to saunter rather than rush, just for now?

3. **Nurture in nature.** Mother Earth always has a way of comforting and healing us when we allow her. Walk out your door and head to the closest gathering of trees, water, or meadow that you can find. No iPod, headphones, or conversation. Look. Listen. Smell. Feel. Be one with nature and allow her grace to fill you up and bring you home. BREATHE in Life and remember who you are and what is true.

Whatever we are thinking and feeling in the moment are our predominant points of attraction. When we consciously shift our focus back to ourselves and our role in any situation, we can see the seduction of evil and release from it. We are free to choose how we contribute our loving, positive energy to the world.

PONDER THIS

What one action could you take to remove something in your environment that doesn't contribute to your well-being?

....

....

....

....

....

Our Fog Is Temporary

"Being human, we all have fogs roll in around our heart,
and often our lives depend on the quiet courage
to wait for them to clear."

~ Mark Nepo, The Book of Awakening

This past August was a difficult month for me as I acknowledged the dates of my parents' anniversary and that of my Mother's physical death. I found myself held captive in a murky sense of separation.

It reminded me of times when driving in a fog, knowing it is too dangerous not to move, yet terrified of blindly moving forward.

My fog rolled in as a bite of grief like a snapping turtle, unexpected, quick, and sharp. It lay heavy around me like a shroud, tethering me to my thoughts, my memories, and the ache of loss.

Without clarity of sight or the confidence that comes from movement, the world closed slowly in, until there was little space left around me.

I found myself in forced recluse — suffocating, suspended in time and abandoned of direction. Alone, feeling scared, and trapped, yet too exhausted to fight.

Once in a while, I'd glimpse a small patch of sky from a thinning hole in the fog. It was these offerings of sanity that held me up and gave me promise of a clearing.

And then after what seemed to span Lifetimes, I surrendered. Now willing to experience new truths and depleted of fear, I was open to acceptance.

Slowly the fog dissipated. As the path lightened and my way became apparent, I bravely stepped forward ....

PONDER THIS

How has a fog in your Life forced you to be open and
surrender to your new path?

....

....

....

....

....

Walking the Slight Edge

"Simple disciplines repeated over time will
create success, while simple mistakes repeated
over time will create failure."

~ Jeff Olson

Recently, I started a cleanse to help me realign with my mindful eating. It took me six months to become willing to be present and honest with myself. I know what supports my body and I know that sugar and caffeine are just empty placeholders.

Why then do I allow myself to get so far off course?

Losing my positive focus and direction doesn't happen overnight. I get there as an incremental manifestation of my choices over time.

It is *The Slight Edge.*

When I fall out of my routine, I have a tendency to feel overwhelmed and disconnected. I beat myself up for feeling this way and judge myself for not being centered. This may sound silly, yet those negative, critical messages have the power to weed up to choke out my daily well-being. They eventually demand my undivided attention.

When I am feeling especially vulnerable and stressed out, I give in to my need to escape or hide. What I am really running from is my fear and my need to be certain!

This is an old pattern of mine. I look outside myself for the perfect solution to make me feel better and to "help me cope." It's my need for emotional comfort that directs my desperate choice to seek a quick fix.

Prior to May 19, 1988 I filled my emotional holes by obsessing with alcohol and cocaine. In early sobriety my sponsor once asked me if I wanted a bat to make my regular beatings easier for me. That question, along with its image, has served me many times over the years. It is such a visual cue.

As with most quick fixes, the drugs appeared to provide immediate relief. For awhile. Yet the quieting of my punishing thoughts was only temporary.

How can I shift the tides of my focus and climb out of the ruts I've built for myself?

Well, it takes what it takes! When I am sick and tired of being sick and tired, I am ready to make a change. I let go of looking outside of myself for answers. I become willing to believe that I deserve to feel better and be happy.

I make a decision to take responsibility for myself and the quality of my Life.

The first step to making any change is becoming aware and accepting of "what is" in the present. I choose to let go of resisting and judging myself ... just for now.

I remind myself that I am only human, and it is our nature to make mistakes. That's how we learn. I reframe the language I use and recognize that the negative messages I hear are from the past.

When I let go of holding onto what I don't want, I create a space within me that is open and receptive. In this present moment I am connected with my highest self and my inner wisdom.

And *it is here ... where I can hear ... the answer to "what's next?"*

PONDER THIS

What pattern are you ready to change
to be free of needing to flog yourself?

....

....

....

....

....

Finding the Balance

"Life is a balance of holding on and letting go!"

~ Rumi

October 11th is my father's birthday. He would have celebrated his 88th year. Instead, we celebrated him by honoring the memories of the love and Life we shared and by missing this wonderful, generous man who filled the great hole in our lives, to overflowing ....

As I headed out into Mother Nature's loving arms, I was filled with a mixture of joy and the familiar pang of ache in my heart. Once again, there lies directly beneath my feet a feather. So close, so real — he touches me, yet not here in the usual way.

Those of us who are familiar with grief recognize that it comes in waves. We experience a compelling need to shout or run or hide. We want to escape and defend ourselves. Finally for little glimmers of time, we settle and accept, even surrender to its embrace …

Our companion, new or longstanding, "our grief."

I've never understood how the world can keep on ticking, keep on pushing around me, as if no one or no thing has changed. It's as if the grief that consumes me is somehow not obvious and the implosion of my heart cannot be seen. Could the confusion and loss of my familiar perception be that insignificant — other than to me?

To find some solace and direction, my sister Lynne and I took a class at Mile High Church from Dr. Patty Luckenbach. During *Grief as a Spiritual Teacher,* Dr. Patty offered us a new concept, a mantra of explanation for this experience. Whether I thrash around in grief's torrid wave or float, spent in my sea of tears, I recognize *grief will ask us to create a new norm.*

Grief, as an energy, has a Life of its own. It is fluid and solid, dark and enlightening, obvious and invisible. It moves in waves or pounces unexpectedly. Cunningly it approaches, slowly rising to the surface. Or just as effectively without warning, it instantly smothers my heart, wrapping it tightly in chains of fear and restriction.

Ignored and repressed, it festers and can ooze out in the most disturbing ways. Then out of control, with both fear and reverence, it becomes threatening and powerful. I have discovered though, that grief, like most wounds, can benefit from attention and care to help it dissipate and heal.

Grief — a shapeshifter — can also be a gift. It reminds me to slow down, to be present, to be compassionate and loving. It creates an infinite space for my forgiveness ....

It is a new way, a new relationship — one that stays with me, patiently waiting for me to notice, to acknowledge and engage.

Grief offers me a new Life process. It allows me to feel, to deal, and ultimately, to heal!

"I've learned that grief can be a slow ache that never seems to stop rising, yet as we grieve, those we love mysteriously become more and more a part of who we are. In this way, grief is yet another song the heart must sing to open the gate of all there is."

~ from *The Book of Awakening*, Mark Nepo

PONDER THIS

When you surrender to your grief, what do you find?

....

....

....

....

....

Reluctant Acceptance

"Resistance to what is creates the suffering."

~ Buddha

It's funny how clarity can come from a restless night's sleep — how every waking moment, I am aware of a relentless mantra of thought, plaguing me with some responsibility to do something about it.

Clearly, this morning the message is about "letting go of the barnwood."

This summer we were fortunate to finally remodel our bathroom. It is the last room to be renovated of the original summer cabin built in the 1940s. We have made cosmetic enhancements to the bathroom over the past 31 years; yet for the most part, it has remained limited and archaic.

I've had a lot of time to imagine how I'd like our bathroom to be. You know some of the best thinking is done in that room. In addition to a larger walk-in shower with a seat, a floor that is level and a two-sink vanity with drawers, my primary focus has been on the decor.

I knew I wanted bold, dramatic, granite stones on the floor of the shower, copper sinks, and lots of rock and wood — barnwood, that is!

Growing up as a "cowgirl" in Colorado, I have always had a fondness for barnwood. I love the stories inherent in the wood, the connection to earth and animals, and the transformation it makes over time.

My grandfather had a farm with a barn in Illinois. My younger sister and I had horses as kids and loved "growing up in a barn." My two Andrew Wyeth prints — *Wind from the Sea* and *Christina's World* — that I've had since I was a teenager are treasures especially because they are framed in barnwood.

Finding the barnwood for this project was quite the task. I discovered the best and closest resource on Craig's List. It had already been a full day when we headed out to locate the barnwood guy's property in Danny's big truck. Though our destination was nearly two hours southeast of Evergreen, Danny, Joe, and I were grateful for an evening without rain and enjoyed the lush green scenery and colorful sky.

Eureka! The Barnwood Guy had a hillside stacked with choices. While battling giant mosquitos and our urgency to complete our mission, we diligently combed through the selection. When the last of the perfect barnwood had been loaded into the truck, we headed home feeling exhausted yet triumphant!

Over the next two weeks the barnwood took shape in desired widths and sections to be ready for use. On schedule, we took delivery on the wood and two beautiful custom doors. I literally danced around in my excitement; my dream was coming true!

Yet I couldn't help but notice the prevalent chemical odor that wafted through the front door as the wood presented itself on the driveway.

Although I tried to make light of it, we could all smell the heavy creosote that had been unleashed by the milling.

We discussed various ways to clean or seal the wood to eliminate the problem. At last we stored the doors in the garage and looked to the morning for answers.

All night I experienced a nagging, aching feeling of impending doom.

Bryan was up by the time I wandered out at 4:15 am. Together we sat on the couch not talking about the thing that laid heavy on our hearts.

I finally shared about the night I had and my major concerns regarding the odor. From his iPad, Bryan quickly shared with me the nasty facts he had learned about creosote.

What a relief it was to hear the gravity of this information. There was nothing left to hold onto! There were no more questions to be asked.

I allowed myself to have a brief meltdown complete with tears while releasing a mixture of anger, frustration, and disappointment.

I had to just let go!

The truth was that this beautiful barnwood could only be used outside and that was that. The truth freed me of my resistance, allowed me to accept the situation, and opened me up to other possibilities.

Eventually I chose rough-cut cedar to make its stand in our bathroom. Though it's been a process, its fresh, earthy, woody aroma has helped me to celebrate the joy that comes from acceptance.

PONDER THIS

What have you reluctantly let go of that opened you up to the joy of acceptance?

....

....

....

....

....

Letting Go Is a Process

"I never felt a pain that didn't bear a blessing."

~ Gene Knudson Hoffman

My sisters and I shared a special week together in the fall spreading our mother's and father's ashes throughout Arizona and Colorado. We specifically chose to visit all their favorite places to celebrate their Life and the love they had for each other.

Our sojourn began at Phoenix Junior College where Dad really started his basketball career and where he first fell in love with the desert climate.

Since the basketball court wasn't readily available, we cracked open "the box of Dad" while standing on home plate of the baseball field. While the maintenance guy watched us from afar, we scooped up handfuls and sent Dad to the winds as we spun around in pirouettes.

I swear I could hear him laughing at our brazen antics. It was a good start. The release had begun.

Next was their home in Scottsdale. We showered a bit of Dad into his beloved patio fountain and at the base of the "shedless olive tree" he had planted for Mother.

We initiated Mom's release by sending her to hover over the desert path where she'd taken thousands of daily walks over the years. Free now, she could choose to continue to sort, soothe, and celebrate her Life if she wanted.

It was on our way to Sedona where my melancholy mood set in. I was taking my turn riding in the back seat, and my sisters and I had been recounting stories about Mom and Dad and our times in Sedona.

Out of nowhere I was hit by an overwhelming sense of loss and missing them. With huge tears tumbling uncontrollably down my cheeks, I exclaimed how surreal this all was and how I desperately wished they could be with us now.

Whether someone said something or I was given a not-so-gentle nudge, I don't remember. But at that moment, I glanced down on the floorboard behind the driver's seat, and there sat "Dad in his box" and "Mother in her gallon Ziplock."

I said as much. My sisters and I laughed so hard and long that we had to make an unscheduled potty stop.

Sedona is truly a sacred place of vortex, healing energy, and sweet memories with our parents. We shared their ashes with the spirits of Oak Creek and with precious stones placed along the Native American labyrinth.

We left Arizona — each a little lighter, more connected, and at peace.

Our next destination was Boulder, Colorado. Coming from Indiana and Illinois, our parents had met, fallen in love, and begun their 62 years together on the University of Colorado campus.

Initially meeting on a double date, Dad thought Mom had a cocky walk and was a little too sure of herself. Mom was equally impressed by Dad's ambitious-yet-humble nature.

From there we continued to share our parents' ashes throughout Colorado. As we headed west, we stopped at the Genesee overlook where Dad gave Mom his fraternity pin. Though no I-70 existed in the 40's, the majestic view of the Rocky Mountains, even then, took their breath away.

We continued west to Vail and Avon. We walked along Gore Creek and remembered our numerous strolls along this river with Mother at the lead.

We hiked around the Walking Mountains Science Center and sprinkled ashes on a stone plaque that is there to honor our mother.

We ate at all our favorite restaurants and enjoyed a reprieve at the local bookstore in Edwards.

Each of us shed some tears; yet being together, honoring our parents in this way, softened the reality of our loss and nurtured the gratitude and love we have for each other.

The following spring we took the last of Mom's ashes back to her hometown of Oregon, Illinois. Growing up, we girls rode the train overnight with Mother to visit our grandparents, aunt and uncle, and cousins. We had stayed for weeks during the summer and learned about lightning bugs, the song of the Whippoorwill, and humidity.

This trip we stayed at a bed and breakfast and took Mom for one last time to the places of our favorite memories. We began at Lowden State Park where the great cement statue of Chief Blackhawk towers over the treetops, keeping a watchful eye up the Rock River.

White Pines Park was our last stop. Here the river flows back and forth over the park road regulating the flow of traffic as each car fords the stream. And what fond memories we have of finally sitting down to enjoy the family-style breakfasts they served in the lodge on Sundays.

As we released the last of Mom's ashes, I felt a sense of closure on a time of innocence and a shift in the memories of my childhood.

The time spent with Uncle Rog and our cousins made for a bittersweet visit. It fanned the joy of our memories and at the same time triggered new layers of grief ....

Completing the "LeSue Ash Tour" gave me a fuller understanding and acceptance of the cycle of Life.

By honoring and letting go of the physical elements of my parents, I felt free to embrace our true and everlasting bond.

PONDER THIS

What personal blessing have you received through

surrendering to an aspect of your Life that was painful?

....

....

....

....

....

Claim Your Freedom

"You find freedom inside, nowhere else.
In the heart of every human being
is that one space which is free, which is filled with peace,
and which is filled with love."

~ Prem Rawat

Freedom is a manifestation of the process of change. It is a concept that recognizes the experience we have when we release from our lives something we don't want.

Many of us resist letting go of anything we don't want. It is more comfortable and safe to stay with the familiar, no matter how oppressive it might be.

Freedom comes when we let go of our belief that we are limited, restricted, or unworthy.

When we focus on what we do want, we can dissolve our imaginary chains. Courageously we can step forward to liberate ourselves from habits of judgment and resistance.

We let go of needing to punish ourselves or blame others for the ruts of unhappiness we've created.

Awareness is the key ....

When I review my Life, its great gifts and blessings, I can see that *only good* has come to me every time I've surrendered my need for control.

I recognize that left unchecked, my ego continues to gather evidence to show me just how unsafe and undeserving I *must be.*

Though this is not the truth!

Years ago I created my Signature Coaching System to give me and my clients a simple, yet effective, structure for processing negative energies and for giving them a way to dissipate from our bodies.

A.S.E.R.T. — my five-step process — is a declaration of intention. It is a commitment to ownership, to demonstrating personal responsibility. It is a structured way to move from our search for outside fixes to a new relationship in communion with self.

A.S.E.R.T. = CLAIM YOUR FREEDOM! CLAIM YOUR LIFE!

Awareness — When activated, "see" and identify limiting beliefs, suppressed feelings, destructive habits, and sabotaging behavior patterns. Once you become aware, it is impossible to retreat back to ignorance.

Shift focus — Make a conscious choice to make what you have seen the center of your interest, to concentrate and pay particular attention to it, to give it permission to reveal itself further. Acknowledgement is a universal olive branch.

Engage inner dialogue — Center yourself, inquire within. Listen and *be* open and receptive to whatever feelings, energies, answers, or insights might surface. Direct self-inquiry with specific questions. *Be* enlightened by your own wisdom.

Release — Allow and accept what is, then give it permission to go, to move out, to dissipate in energetic intensity. *Be* liberated from the power and control these non-serving energies have had over you and your Life.

Transform — Create and embrace new ways of *being*. Implement choices. Initiate forward movement. *Be* confident, clear, and directed to your next right step. *Be* empowered to successfully manifest from this new free space — your joy and purpose!

PONDER THIS

What unwanted behaviors are you ready to BE FREE of?
List the first 3 you became aware of.

....

....

....

....

GRATITUDE

Live in the state of rejoicing!

"Gratitude unlocks the fullness of life.
It turns what we have into enough, and more.
It turns denial into acceptance,
chaos to order, confusion to clarity.
It can turn a meal into a feast,
a house into a home,
a stranger into a friend.
Gratitude makes sense of our past,
brings peace for today,
and creates a vision for tomorrow."

- Melody Beattie

GRATITUDE
Live in the state of rejoicing!

Trust Your Good

The Art of Acknowledgment

A Thankful Voice

Action Speaks

Gratitude for You

Success in Gratitude

Trust Your Good

"Everlasting happiness is based on a basic trust that your Life is not happening to you; it's happening for you."

~ Dr. Robert Holden

How very simple Life might be if we could trust that everything really does happen for our highest and greatest good. When we deem what is happening as positive or pleasant, it is easy to believe this quote from Dr. Robert Holden.

But what about when our lives seem to be catapulting out of control? Or when the other shoe has definitely dropped and there seems to be no light at the end of our tunnel?

How could these seemingly negative or challenging situations be to our benefit?

All of us experience Life. And Life is comprised of events, situations, relationships, and circumstances.

How we respond to our Life creates the quality of our experience.

181

Take a moment to conduct a quick review of your Life. Focus on remembering those big things, those monumental shifts in your journey. What do you notice being the *end result* of the upheaval, trauma, or illness? Where has this experience taken you?

Again the quality of our experience rests in our thoughts and the choices we make. If we are stuck in looking outside ourselves for validation, love, or success, we will find the world's offering always falls short.

If we look for someone or something to blame for our unhappiness, we will continue to attract more evidence to justify why we are so unhappy. And in the meantime, we are incapable of seeing any of the gifts or support that is being presented to us.

Living from a victim's consciousness fuels the belief that we've been singled out to suffer: Life is unfair and we are being punished.

When we come from a place of gratitude we experience a Life of trust. We slow down our focus to the present where we can recognize ways we are, indeed, being taken care of.

We live from a firm belief in the reliability, the strength, and the truth of Life to care for us. We experience faith and confidence in whatever is happening to offer us an opportunity to see, to choose, and to grow.

"When the bird lands on a twig, it does not worry that it might break,
it trusts instead, in its ability to fly."

~ Anonymous

PONDER THIS

What is one of the greatest gifts you've been given
through an initial hardship?

....

....

....

....

....

The Art of Acknowledgment

"Nothing builds self-esteem and self-confidence
like accomplishment."

~ Thomas Carlyle

Most of us massively produce all day long. We complete multiple tasks and manage to juggle our endless responsibilities. We continuously revise our schedules in an effort to make progress at attaining our goals.

We've become masters on the path of *human doing-ness* and cleverly strive to squeeze into each moment, our best (if not perfect) performance. It is an intensive exercise of generating more and keeping up the pace.

Yet at the end of the day, despite what we might have accomplished, do any of us really celebrate ourselves for a job well done or a great day lived?

Accomplishment is not enough!

For us to experience joy and fulfillment in our lives we must develop a consistent practice of something else.

We must learn the *art of acknowledgment*.

We must practice giving attention to and deeming value for "whatever it is" that we've accomplished.

We certainly practice and can reiterate numerous accountings of our failures and where we've fallen short. Learning to slow down to assess the mini milestones of our lives is about *choosing a new direction* for our focus.

What if we recognize and praise even the small things we do?

Could we celebrate each time we *show up* for an appointment we've made? Better yet, one we've cancelled, then rescheduled?

Could we acknowledge *following through* on a task that we've been procrastinating?

Could it matter to us and be valued, how we show up for Life everyday and with what attitude?

Accomplishment alone does not change how we feel about ourselves and our capabilities. It is what we think and how we feel about our accomplishment that fuels our self-esteem.

Ever notice how good you feel about yourself upon completing a task that's been bugging you? Like taking out the trash, clearing the piles on your desk, or picking up that trash that keeps greeting you on the path?

Or it could be a huge accomplishment. Advocate for yourself. Support a cause. Make an apology.

Acknowledging the things you do, giving yourself credit for *beginning, making progress, or finishing something* is like giving yourself the proverbial "pat on the back!"

Who doesn't love that feeling of being acknowledged?

Acknowledgment — It is this personal practice that builds trust and confidence in ourselves and empowers us to see and then take our next right step.

PONDER THIS

What three personal accomplishments are you now willing to acknowledge?

....

....

....

....

....

A Thankful Heart

"Gratitude is the memory of the heart."

~ Jean Baptiste Massieu

Since I was a kid, I have enjoyed writing as a way to express myself. Journaling, jotting down quotes, and recording my personal insights have always brought me home — home to where my heart remembers, home to the present.

The format of an acrostic has been a favorite of mine — a poem, the first letters of each line spelling out a word. I love the structure it provides to focus my thoughts and script my message. As I turn my attention to the present season, I "see" the word *grateful*.

GRATEFUL

Gratitude is a choice, an attitude, a practice. It is a "state of being," which has its roots in the present — where God is.

Running water invites me to be present. In taking my shower or washing my hands, I focus on honoring those who cannot experience this luxury. I close my eyes and savor the activity in gratitude.

Acceptance illuminates and expands my present consciousness. It unleashes my resistance and allows me to flow effortlessly in the rhythm of Life.

Trust is the venue where truth shines light. It's a place on a dark path where I can stand in faith. It is my memory of connection and the voice of my inner wisdom.

Energy = Life. Spirit. Movement. Passion. Power!

Freedom to be authentically me. Free to show up, contribute, and receive love from my family, friends, furry companions, and Mother Nature.

Unlimited. Infinite possibilities and potential. I create my Life how I want it to be from my own perspective of the present moment.

Love is all there is right here, right now. Abundant, consistent, and unconditional. And because you're right here reading this now, I hold you gratefully in my heart!

PONDER THIS

When you think of being grateful,
what does your heart want you to see?

....

....

....

....

....

Action Speaks

"Thankfulness is the beginning of gratitude.
Gratitude is the completion of thankfulness.
Thankfulness may consist merely of words.
Gratitude is shown in acts."

~ Henry F. Amiel

Many of us jump right into the busy-ness of our holidays. The shopping, preparing, scheduling, and traveling dictates our actions while expectation and emotion appear to dominate our thoughts.

We forget to preserve and honor the true meaning of our celebrations. We lose focus in the human doing rather than our human being-ness.

During the next holiday, let us consciously demonstrate our gratitude by being present, by slowing ourselves down, and by actively listening to each other.

May we participate in "acts of thanks-giving" by honestly expressing our acknowledgement, gratitude, and love ....

PONDER THIS

What acts of thanksgiving could you express today?

....

....

....

....

....

Gratitude for You

*"At times our own light goes out and is rekindled
by a spark from another person.
Each of us has cause to think with deep gratitude
of those who have lighted the flame within us."*

~ Albert Schweitzer

I especially like this quote from Albert Schweitzer. It reminds me of the immeasurable influence and power each of us has to lift another.

When Life events knock us down, we lose our balance and at times our ability to trust that we will recover.

We can feel swallowed up by grief or lost and fearful in our confusion.

Yet everywhere we turn someone is ready to support us, to remind us of the truth, or to share their light and love with us in the moment.

Whether it is a patient ear, an empathetic message, or a loving hug, others offer a constant energy to affirm that we are not alone, that Life is good.

Past, Present, and Future! I have so much to be grateful for ....

Today I celebrate with gratitude — the teachers, friends, and family who continue to help me step forward into the light.

Thank you for "being the spark" that reignites my heart again and again.

PONDER THIS

Who in your Life reignites your heart?

....

....

....

....

....

Success in Gratitude

"Without gratitude, you may focus only
on what's lacking in your life,
rather than what you appreciate.
Gratitude keeps you optimistic,
and evidence shows that optimism improves your health."

~ Lissa Rankin, M.D.

It is the New Year, and January is already over!

What emotion does this statement conjure up for you? Some of us experience a twinge of panic. Whether we made New Year's resolutions or just pretend we did, this opportunity for a fresh start, to change something in our lives and the pressured hype to be successful can be a powerful impetus for our feeling frustrated and disappointed.

When did the turning over of a new year become more important than *living each day to the fullest*?

Whatever happened to *"Today is the first day of the rest of your Life?"* Many of us remember that slogan and the smiley face of the same era that reminded us to *"Have a good day!"*

Changing for the better is our preferred, positive direction. Yet when we set our focus on someone else's plan or version of what "better" looks like, we set ourselves up for chasing the elusive butterfly.

We separate ourselves from our own power, guidance, and direction. We waste the promise of infinite possibilities. In order to feel better, we put our faith into the *dangling carrots* beyond our reach just outside of us.

Let's shift gears here for a minute.

What if you turned your attention within?

What if you decide to stop chasing anything?

What if you slowed down a bit to listen for your own wisdom and to see your own direction?

What if you focus on feeling and *being* grateful?

Gratitude is the acknowledgement of something greater than ourselves, not outside of ourselves. Gratitude is the broader perspective, the *big picture.*

Our gratitude illuminates our part in the greater whole and assures us — always — that we are not alone ....

PONDER THIS

Make a list of the top 7 aspects of your Life
for which you are grateful?

....

....

....

....

....

....

....

Make a commitment to focus on these each day.

Allow all the other stuff to slough off from lack of attention.

Celebrate all the successes that come to you daily
when you live in gratitude!

TO MY READERS

Thank you friend for joining me in this journey to ponder
a higher consciousness and deeper meaning of Life.

May you revive your valiant warrior and renew
your relationship with courage.

May you exercise your power to choose in every aspect of your Life
— mindfully directing your attention to that which you value.

May you clarify and recommit to your personal integrity
and proudly revere your expression of truth.

May you cultivate daily from your heart center
— your kindness, acceptance, and love.

May you consciously choose to create and
communicate from this Now moment.

May you celebrate your Freedom each time you let
go of something that no longer serves you.

May you live in a state of Gratitude.

And may you trust that you are not alone and
that all of Life is worth celebrating!

With love & light,

Jani McCarty

"Do your little bit of good where you are.
It's those little bits of good put together
that overwhelm the world."

- Desmond Tutu

ABOUT THE ILLUSTRATOR

Gail Folsom Jennings is an artist and illustrator who lives in the mountains of Colorado. She attended the University of Colorado Denver and Rocky Mountain College of Art and Design where she earned BFA degrees in painting, illustration, and graphic design. Also a Certified Botanical Illustrator, Gail loves to roam the nearby forests, creeks and meadows to study the myriad of native plants of the region. GailFolsomJennings.com

ABOUT THE AUTHOR

Jani McCarty is an author, speaker, transformational teacher and coach. Her genuine interest and compassionate presence have a way of making you feel good about yourself.

She generously shares the wisdom that comes from over 35 years of her own transformational journey to help you remember the truth of who you are! Offering profound insights through intuitive reflection, she guides you to reconnect with your path, power, and purpose.

Her Claim Your Freedom structured process inspires you to reach deep within to iIlluminate sabotaging behaviors, liberate the constraints of negative thinking, and celebrate Life's abundance as your highest self.

Since 2009, Jani has focused on teaching, coaching, and partnering with others in their transformational journeys. She is a Transformational Life Coach®, Heal Your Life© Coach, successful entrepreneur, and celebrates 30 years recovery from alcohol and drug addiction.

Celebrate! an interactive journey thru Life's invitations… is her first published book. Other published works include "Griefs Sacred Passage" Wisdom from the Wild Heart and "Be Here Now" 111 Morning Meditations. She can be found in the Spiritual Leaders Directory 2018.

Jani lives in the foothills of Evergreen CO with her husband Bryan and their dog Charlie. She celebrates Life with family and friends, being in nature and with her horse PeanutButter.

janimccarty.com

CPSIA information can be obtained
at www.ICGtesting.com
Printed in the USA
FSHW02n1946160718
50584FS